DR. STEPHEN SHAPIRO is Director of Vo
Counseling Service of Rockland County, New
York. HILARY RYGLEWICZ is a Senior Mei
Health Worker at the Rockland County Community
Mental Health Center in New York. She and
Stephen Shapiro are the authors of
Trusting Yourself, also published by
Prentice-Hall, Inc.

Feeling Safe: Making Space for the Self

Stephen Shapiro
Hilary Ryglewicz

A SPECTRUM BOOK

PRENTICE-HALL, INC., Englewood Cliffs, New Jersey

Library of Congress Cataloging in Publication Data

Shapiro, Stephen.
  Feeling safe.

  (A Spectrum Book)
  Includes index.
  1. Security (Psychology). 2. Self. 3. Anxiety.
4. Psychology, Pathological. I. Ryglewicz, Hilary, joint author. II. Title
BF575.S35S48   157'.3'2   76-13910
ISBN 0-13-314005-9
ISBN 0-13-313999-9 pbk.

Copyright 1976 by Prentice-Hall, Inc., Englewood Cliffs, New Jersey

All rights reserved. No part of this
book may be reproduced in any form
or by any means without permission
in writing from the publisher.

A Spectrum Book

10 9 8 7 6 5 4 3 2 1
Printed in the United States of America

Prentice-Hall International, Inc., *London*
Prentice-Hall of Australia Pty. Limited, *Sydney*
Prentice-Hall of Canada, Ltd., *Toronto*
Prentice-Hall of India Private Limited, *New Delhi*
Prentice-Hall of Japan, Inc., *Tokyo*
Prentice-Hall of Southeast Asia Pte. Ltd., *Singapore*

Contents

PREFACE vi

INTRODUCTION 1

ONE
IMAGES OF SAFETY 7

TWO
UNSAFE SPACE:
NIGHTMARE, CHILDHOOD, AND PSYCHOSIS 22

THREE
UNSAFE SPACE:
ANXIETY, AND FANTASY: THE WAKING DREAM   37

FOUR
UNSAFE SPACE: THE FLIGHT FROM THE SELF   48

FIVE
UNSAFE SPACE: THE SPLITTING OF THE SELF   61

SIX
MAKING THE SELF: SEPARATION AND INTEGRATION   78

SEVEN
THE RHYTHMS OF THE SELF   98

EIGHT
WAKING FROM THE SOCIAL NIGHTMARE   114

READINGS   147

Preface

There is only one horror story, and it begins: *A monster came into the house.* There is only one ending for such a story, and that is when the house is made safe again. Until that is done, the monsters reign, and the life in the house is bent to placate, flee, combat, or contain them.

We are all afraid of monsters, and we each have some monsters to fear, in our worlds and in our selves. Most of us also have a sense, perhaps a nearly forgotten sense, of what it is to feel safe. But for many of us the fabric of safety is damaged, stained with anxiety, creased with conflicts, riddled with warning signals. For many of us the sense of safety is fragile and fleeting, and for some of us there is no safe home in this world. For some of us, the daylight world is shot through with nightmare fears.

A spectre stalks our walking hours; it is the fear that our nightmares will be realized. We fear our own dying in car crashes, cancer operations, heart attacks, poisoned air, muggings, sudden street battles, strokes of sheer chance. We fear rape, persecution and exclusion, war, exploitation and helplessness in all its forms. And it happens. We read our nightmares in the newspapers and see them on television. Some of us recover a sense of safety only by closing our mind's eye.

We inherit a world made by fear. If we can understand how fear works, we have a chance to remake that world, little by little, starting with ourselves, and to learn to feel safe within ourselves, with others, and in the world. Otherwise, we will remain frozen by fear, and we will reproduce a world of fear.

Knowing who we are is the way out of fear—of ourselves, of others, and of social institutions. Because they are made of us, just as we are made of them. All the monsters—from those that haunt a child's sleep, to the fire-breathing, clawed dragons of myth, to child-abusing parents, to the ovens of Auschwitz—are produced by the human unconscious. They are made of fear. Dreams, stories, family life, and history are given nightmare forms by our own fears. Nothing is so cruel as fear, not even death. And only two processes are strong enough to reduce and contain fear. Those two processes are: knowing and loving.

Feeling safe means, first, gaining trust in one's capacity to set limits for bad experience. This trust makes it possible to still the voices of anxiety and to open up to experience, to unveil one's eyes, to swallow, to breathe in, to hear, to unbind the knots of the heart and the restraints upon sexual love, to let go of the plugs of fear that screen and block the penetrations of feeling.

Feeling safe means the capacity for undivided absorption in being, whether in gazing at a tree, involving oneself in reverie or rapture, absorbing oneself in a creative task, or making a gesture of love. Unsafe being is shadowed and dark; progress into feeling safe is marked by stages of brightening and radiance, of clarity and color, of emerging pattern and design. The terrified feeling that monsters lurk in the darkness and *anything can happen* changes into a rhythmic security of understanding. In the light of this understanding, the processes of the self, of others, and of social groups are seen more clearly. In this clear perception, we are able to look compassionately at ourselves and at others, and we are free to respond fully to what we see.

Above all, feeling safe makes involvement possible. When we are not afraid, we are free to be in touch and involved with the organizations and people "out there," as well as with our own thoughts and feelings. In one sense, the world outside is as safe as our inner world allows it to be. In another sense, feeling safe depends on safe social being. Feeling safe is an experience. Being safe is a function of our social relationships and institutions.

Being safe means being held—by individuals who know us and care about us, by groups that stimulate us and receive from us, and by networks, or communities, that offer us the opportunity to relate to social

Preface

life in a constructive way. Feeling safe means feeling held, contained within limits, yet free to move to our own rhythms and to respond to the rhythms of others. It means feeling that we can contain ourselves and protect ourselves, and therefore that we can dare to share our thoughts and feelings and needs with others whom we can trust. When we feel able to trust, we know that other people are not monsters, and that our own feelings and wishes are not monsters hidden in the house of the self.

This book is about the house of the self and about the monsters that roam its rooms and assault its walls. It is also about the process of psychotherapy—a process of naming the monsters and shrinking them to human size and powers, a process of freeing the house of the self and reclaiming its rooms for human use.

There is another, larger house to be freed, and that is the social world we inhabit—for some, an expanding world of many rooms, rich with color and light; and for others a space that is cramped and barren, crowded with burdens and damaged furniture, worn with the tracks of duty and impulse, disintegrating daily for lack of rebuilding and repair.

Neither the inner world nor the world outside can be entirely safe for any human being. Growth and change involve risk. But we can make ourselves a place to stand and can derive a viable sense of safety from knowing the world, caring for each other, knowing ourselves.

Introduction

Our purpose in this book is to show how we develop, both in relation to our critical stages of development, and as we are encouraged, inhibited, or threatened in those stages of development by our social containers—the family, the group, the political form, the cultural mode. The power to play organizes the world of the child—if the child is not frozen in terror. Similarly, the adolescent learns to voice his concerns and to match his words with acts, if he is given space—with limits. And the young adult learns to explore, confident in his physical and social skills—if the parents, the peer group, and the political economy do not exclude or reject him. Creativity in mid-life depends on previous stages of growth.

The self, the family, and the political form are involved in complex reciprocal interactions which, at our present stage of development, *idealize empathy, but practice scapegoating*. The world has been so unsafe, and our defenses against vulnerability so rigidly canalized, that we find ourselves using our defensive systems instead of our human capacities. As individuals, families, groups, and nations, we allow our defense budgets to become inflated by our fantasies.

We experience our identity in three phases: first as a product of family space; secondly as a product of social space. Then, if we struggle hard and find supportive networks, we are able to transcend our schizoid mechanism—our neurosis—as well as the rigid role definitions of our local culture and discover ourselves, not as reactive gestures of defense or as comparative images, but as intelligent rhythmic energies, able to move and create and love. If we do not grow into this third phase, feelings of frustration, rage, envy, and spite become barriers to empathic relations with our own selves and with others. We look for scapegoats; we idealize; we punish; we split our mind, body, and feelings; we compete with shadows. For the unrealized self, no space is safe.

Feeling safe means, as we shall see, knowing that we do not cast shadows, that we do not inadvertently say, show, or do unintended things or give unconscious messages; and it means being able to trust ourselves to perceive the messages of others, and to act appropriately in our own interests.

The basic human problem is that we do not see ourselves or one another clearly. The reason for this is threefold: We perceive ourselves as victims of what we endured in the past and project that expectation of victimage; we are unclear about the separateness of the self and the otherness of the other; and we have difficulty focusing on our own role in any interaction, tending to feel we say and do differently from what we actually say and do. This position of confusion constantly generates new confusions in our relationships. Being clear about ourselves and others means knowing that: we are *not* victims; that others *are* who they are, independent of their relation to us; and that we must alter our own behavior to get the results we seek. Being unclear about self and other means that on some level we resent being born and so not accept the conditions of our being in the world.

Feeling safe means overcoming feelings of victimage and the floating rage of the victim; knowing who others are; and knowing how to play with the possibilities of our own creative action. Basically, this book explores the nightmares of psychic, family and social life, and their interference with our capacity to grow through play.

Play is serious. Play is the realm of the possible, experienced in safety. Play enables us to discharge tensions, to integrate our own body functions, to understand other bodies, and to create an interplay between the inner and outer world. Play helps us to sort out objects, experiences, and ideas, and it helps us to make new combinations. Play is neither planned, controlled, nor out of control. It does not end with childhood, but remains the domain of action that remains fluid. But this domain is not open to us when we are

Introduction

living the role of the victim, or when every step out of a repetitive pattern of action and feeling makes us fear for our lives.

We cannot satisfy all our needs by being still, and therefore we must involve ourselves with the world. We are ambivalent about this involvement, however, and would prefer to withdraw into a perfection of self-sufficient self-involvement, that is, into the safety of the womb. Yet need pulls and pushes us to recognize a world which frustrates and satisfies us. Reluctantly, we begin to map that world, distorting it egocentrically whenever and wherever we can do so without being killed by our illusions.

We feel most safe when we feel the world is all *for* us—or when we feel we have the whole world safe inside us. But this is a false form of safety, because we cannot arrest change or prevent collision with the implacable otherness of the world, its invincible separateness from the image of our desire. We do not surrender easily, however. We *will* project the world in our own image—as an ideal or as a hell—confusing image, appearance, and real process—until our bruises compel us to learn the difference between our ideas and our experience.

All our difficulties, as persons and as members of groups, stem from this tension between our private imagery and our memberships in public worlds, which we may distort by our projections, but which are not made into our images. Fire will burn us; loves will leave us; Vietnamese will fight us. Some of us learn to adapt our maps to experience, instead of fighting to turn rock, time, and others into mirrors of our needs. Those who make good maps become lamps for the rest of us struggling in the fog. Others simply mirror our own confusion.

As with maps, so with clocks. Infants demand immediate gratification and, if deprived, hallucinate the object of their desire. Impatience is this struggle between the inner clock of desire and the time of clocks in others not attuned to our own needs. At other stages of the life cycle, we try, as individuals and as cultures, to freeze time, to remove the hands of the clock and to deny the changes it measures, so that we need not confront the necessities of our own development and our social reality, and so that we may try to deny the inevitability of death, the one monster that finally must destroy the safe house of every self.

Feeling safe is different from imagining ourselves to be safe. Mythmaking about others and the world, which is temporarily reassuring, disorients us and interferes with the maps and models we need in reality. Myths are both ways of understanding the world and ways of distorting it. Such false forms of security obscure true forms. For example, denying, pretending, or whitewashing a situation is not the same as optimism; and clinging to someone or something out of desperation is not the same as love. Repetition of familiar behavior is not the same as understanding one's situation.

We all make mental maps of situations, people, ourselves, interactions. The problem of discriminating between appearance and reality, long the problem of art, philosophy, and religion, is now the politics of everyday life, both for individuals and for nations. We tend to stereotype other races and nations, as well as the other sex and people at different age levels. We generate us/them, good/bad, right/wrong dualisms. These are false forms of security, frail fortresses in which we attempt to hide from the realization that *we* are *them* and *they* are *us,* which, is the real basis of empathy. Empathy is going into the feeling of another person without necessarily approving that feeling. It is recognizing how the other feels, as opposed to "missing the mark" and denying who the other person is.

Because of the way fantasy merges with reality in the perceptions and reactions of groups, the discrimination between fantasy and reality is not a simple one of measuring thought processes against an open, sane social standard. Too often, the paranoid fantasy is true. It is very hard to convince a paranoid Black or woman or child of the fantasy-projective nature of his or her fears when social groups are in fact persecutory and are confirming those fears at every turn. This problem of discrimination of fear and fact is central to personal development. Our need is to perceive clearly, with open hearts—without idealization or denigration. When we can do so, we are then able both to defend ourselves and to open ourselves to others.

As individuals and as a culture, we are always seeking some means of transforming our life in the world. The current contest between transcendental meditation and more esoteric forms of Tantric Buddhism in the psychic questing of Americans for security is a fascinating phenomenon. America is not India or Tibet. We do have much to learn from the profound sacred psychologies of Hinduism and Buddhism—but they may be useful to us only in our own context of family and social relationships. Otherwise, they constitute only one more episode in our national preoccupation with separating ourselves from a corrupt Old World. In quest of Eden, of the New Jerusalem, we delude ourselves with holy ideas while we practice isolation, arrogance and greed—counterfeit versions of our real social selves. Self-deception is endless. Often, we find ourselves trying to become an idealized Other in the very process of seeking our own being. Mystical chic is replacing radical chic.

This American desire to be the idealized Other—the Chosen People—has been a mask for assassination, repression, slavery, racism, and imperialism. We cannot solve our problems by masking them with ideals or sacred rituals. TM for IBM executives will not give us livable communities, any

Introduction

more than LSD will—although both TM and LSD have their therapeutic uses. Buddha and Rama symbolized the caring community; but we must recognize that we cannot import such a community. Rather, we must make one out of our shattered families, our tattered ethics, our ragbag of therapies, our empty churches, our Babel of special vocabularies, our bankrupt cities. In the end, our personal problems are not separable from our social ones. The division of psychic growth from social responsibility is unworkable. As Gandhi said, whoever feels that religion is not involved with politics does not understand religion.

The mind is a crazy monkey and needs to be stilled. Then the real social tasks become clear. When we overcome our private nightmare, we encounter the social nightmare. It is easier to go to the moon, to learn Sanskrit chants, or to love all mankind than it is to overcome the envy in one person or the injustice in one community. The safety of idealized withdrawal is a false form of safety. We are contained by the state, and the values of the state mirror our lowest levels of collective self and family development. Manic ideas, flight in all its forms, and messianic economies merely delude; they do not solve social problems.

Real problems of the life cycle and community are so depressing sometimes, it is easy to daydream: This is not *my* family or world. My real life lies in some ideal time or place, some superreal Nowhere. This is self-rejection and the hatred of reality, the inability to realize that all conditions are the same, as opportunities for constructive work. Here. Now. In English. Our national crisis in childrearing, schooling, and juvenile crime, as well as in the alienation of the elderly and in underemployment, calls for the formation of new social networks and for the revival of citizen participation in schools, mental health, and in a new politics.

Pain, confusion, insecurity and the sense of meaninglessness are intolerable. We seek safe space, safe time, and the sense that things, people, and events fit together in a pattern of some kind. Human understanding of what safety is has undergone three major transformations. First, magic and the gods were invoked as healers, protectors, and social organizers. The safe space of Eden, lost in time, was projected into the afterlife. The need to have immediate protection against external and internal danger and uncertainty—or at least to have faith in such protection—contributed to this continued magical structuring of experience. Second, with the development of industry and medical science, the need to be sheltered and cured changed its focus; industrial production and medical cures became a source of magical hope. The doctrines of human perfectability, endless progress, and the germ theory of disease seemed to promise the descent of heaven to earth.

The failure of both the magical and the technical gods to produce universal security has stimulated a third, ecological form of understanding individual and social behavior. Under the influence of Einstein and Darwin, philosophers like Whitehead tried to formulate actions, thoughts, and feelings as dynamically related, rather than as isolated things. Our perspective is the same; safe space, as a physical, psychological, and social reality is not a fixed place or thing but a process unfolding in space-time.

The self is a dynamic process. Without stimulation, we would die. Without protection from stimulation, we would die. The task of personal development, like the evolution of life and social process, is the maintenance of safe space for vital processes, of a safe rhythm of containing and being contained.

Information—and its comprehension through insight—is essential to the construction of safe space. Without knowing our needs, our position, and the location of social goods and "bads," we are doomed to secret government, subversion, invasion, and self-damage. At every level, from the immune system to growing, to raising children, to governing an organization, we must have the capacity to recognize, discriminate, and regulate influences from the surrounding field. Only then can we clear safe space for the self and for our exchange with others.

Feeling safe is based on trust—in our senses, our judgments, our models of interaction, and our relations with others. This trust is based on having a good clock and a good map, or a map and clock of reachable goods, based on our stage of development and on our relation to our own groups and networks. Trust is based on awareness of our real feeings, our real situations, our real needs and capacities. Trust, in other words, is based on knowing and learning ourselves and each other—a long, confusing process beginning in the dark.

Images of Safety

ONE

> *I just wish there was someplace I could go and think things over, you know?*
> *That was a good time in my life. Everything there was real.*
> *At least now I know, whatever happens, I have myself.*

THE SAFETY OF THE WOMB

Our life begins in a bag of waters. That is the first home for our being, the first source of our nurture—a close, dark, space, hidden in the body of the mother. There we grow, insulated and fed. From there we break out into chaos, hunger, danger.

The womb is our first safe space, and it leaves a deep imprint on the psyche. Without the chance to grow there, we could not live. Yet we can live there only as sojourners. The womb stretches but it can't contain our growth. If we did not burst out, our growth would cease, and the dark bed that was our haven would become our grave.

We are thrust out into a world of shocks and hazards, a confusion of sound and light; and we find our safety in other containments—the sheltering bed, the feeding mother's arms, the rhythms of need and response that hold and lull us. These less certain, more ample havens protect our further growth, allowing us respite from the unbearable flow of stimuli, the mortal threat of unsatisfied need, the painful differentiation of self from the magical, feeding breast. We grow and learn to feel safe in ever more open spaces,

7

ever more complex patterns. But we never cease to need the rhythmic, restorative return to what is easy, what is familiar, what is trusted—even though, if growth goes well, we learn to carry much of the sense of safety within ourselves.

Growth is not easy, and it always involves risk, pain and disappointment. So the womb and the breast persist, as symbols of total gratification, in our fantasies, in our myths, and in our deepest hopes. In fantasy, that was paradise, now lost; that was love, now marred by frustration and demands; that was heaven, perhaps someday to be regained. The religious concept of life between the womb and the grave as a lengthy struggle is also, much of the time, our human experience. Fulfillment is hard-won; needs often go unmet; the fruit does not fall easily from the trees. The human being is a complex balance, vulnerable to stress and to many dangers. How natural, then, to remember an image of sanctuary and perfect contentment, whether it wears the shape of the womb itself or of some life space more recent or more remote—a childhood seen as carefree, an early romance, an imagined Garden of Eden. Like Platonists, we seek in the shadows of reality the gratifying forms of the ideal.

But in fact we could not fit into the womb again; nor could we even revisit childhood without finding its rooms shrunken, shabbier than our golden images. Childhood, even if happy, is unrecoverable; the early love is soon outgrown; and nothing was quite as we remember it anyway. We may encounter again, in priceless moments, the legendary happiness of a sense of union with another being or our own universe. But these experiences are fleeting in their very nature; they stand out luminously against a background of many colors that are paler or more shadowed, and they are only fragments in our adult happiness. We remain separate; we remain ourselves; and the environment in which we seek our satisfactions is more hazardous than the bag of waters, less predictable than a mother's arms, more variegated than any dream of paradise. These waters are uncharted, barely fathomed, and we must learn and make our own pockets of security, our safe channels, our points of orientation, our breeding grounds—all of which are perpetually shifting, often slightly and sometimes greatly.

THE "SAFETY" OF ROLES AND RITUALS

Safety for us, then, cannot mean anything simple, insulated, placid, or static, although sometimes we seek it in a variety of womb-like enclosures. These may be roles, ritualized patterns, sets of defenses, preoccupations, or constraints laid upon the self in order to avoid the possibility of danger.

Some people overinvest money and attention in insurance, burglar alarms, karate courses, health foods, or safety belts—as if ferreting out all specific threats, and mustering against them all the techniques of protection, could overcome the basic contingency of our existence. Some people seek the sense of safety by trying to keep everything the same; clinging to a traditional role, trying to do all things the way mother and father did them, keeping experience confined to a narrow world, mistrusting anything which represents change.

Many of us, while not clinging in this way to the past, cling to constricted versions of the present. Many people identify themselves so fully with their roles—as wives, as workers, as members of a social class or an ethnic group or a neighborhood or a group of friends—that all experience is channeled into these forms. Many of us are locked into a limited concept of ourselves, not venturing beyond our own familiar patterns, our accustomed level of self-esteem, or our accumulated experience of what it is safe to feel, think and so. Some of us limit ourselves to fantasies about the future, for we tend to feel safer in fantasy than in reality, which always carries its possibility of the failure of our hopes and our efforts.

These patterns are experiential wombs. Their protection binds and constricts the self. Life in these terms is like living in a house with certain rooms closed off: The space is cramped, yet everyone uses the rooms already furnished with safe habits, and the others remain empty.

These are the patterns that sometimes produce the agonizing upheavals at mid-life or sooner, as the person begins to see his life already enclosed, already in the perspective of death. A man in his early forties, depressed for no reason he knows, says: *I get up, I go to work, I go home, I watch TV, I keep thinking that there must be something more to life, you know? I have no complaints, I have a nice home, a good wife, good children, good job, no complaints. But when I wake up in the morning, I don't want to get out of bed.* Women, gathered to share their feelings, talk about their broken marriages. One says: *I always tried to be the perfect wife to my husband. But that wasn't what he wanted.* Another: *I wanted to be my husband's lover and his friend; but I was always too busy being his wife.* Another, facing herself for the first time, says: *I want to be a new person now. But how can you be a person if no one loves you?* And a fourth says: *I did everything I thought I should, just the way my mother did it. I thought I was being a good wife, but I was really a mother to my husband.*

These are people who have lived in roles, in the patterns of safe behavior they had been taught, only to become prisoners of those roles. Breaking away from such patterns is like a new, more gradual birth—the birth of the self. Like all change, it has elements of terror, and we may ask, like the prisoner in the story of the Corsican Brothers, *But what will I do on the outside?* Sometimes this terror even drives people into more constricted patterns, like those of the divorcee who gives up all her old friends, of the disabled man who loses his job and takes to drink, or of the widower who moves in with his married daughter, even though he is still in middle age.

For our habitual roles, constricting as they may be, fit us like a comfortable skin. We know where this garment binds and where it will stretch to accommodate our familiar movements. To be without this skin of habit is to be naked, cold, and afraid; to be unguided by habit feels unsafe.

These patterns are ways of trying to avoid *risk,* to avoid *danger,* to avoid *threat,* to avoid the possibility of loss and pain. The survivor of a broken romance who avoids further involvements; the woman who fails a driver's test and never tries again; the man who would like to change his career but puts it off until "someday"; the wife who never lays down the dish towel to put on a sexy nightgown—these are people avoiding the possibility of failure, rejection, or disappointment. Their motto is: *Nothing ventured, nothing lost.* The possible rebuff, the potential insult to the ego, is felt as a real danger to the self; the person stays instead on the safe, familiar path which limits growth.

To a degree, these methods "work"; our habitual patterns do hold us in a kind of safety. Insuring ourselves against one kind of threat—staying off the streets at night, keeping regular hours, watching our investments, fulfilling others' expectations—we may feel an increased security, a sense of somehow being in control of what happens in our lives. Limiting our experience, so that it remains within the boundaries of what we are used to, actually does screen out thought, feeling and experience which could make us feel anxious, threatened, or in conflict.

Sometimes the nature of the threat is not as it appears on the surface. The young person avoiding relationships, the wife or husband avoiding sex, may be afraid, not of failure, but of success; the danger may not be an anticipated rebuff but the possibility of close emotional contact, which may involve conflict and anxiety on an unconscious level. The wife who avoids the driver's test may actually be avoiding the independence involved in learning to drive, which in turn might threaten the security of her marriage. We are sensitive animals with finely developed antennae; we are able to sense threat and danger from a great distance—sometimes, unfortunately, at so great a distance that we shut out the threatening possibility without being able to see clearly what it is, what it means, and how it could be handled.

Yet the "safety" which is gained through the avoidance of risk and change is an illusory safety. Like the protection of the womb, it is secure but constrictive, and cannot allow enough space for the expanding self to grow.

The capacities for dealing with threat, risk, and change are not developed unless there is opportunity for their gradual growth through progressive stages of experience. Muscles which are not used cannot develop; they can only atrophy. Our mental and emotional capacities, too, can be enlarged only through their exercise with relation to our experience. When we do not allow ourselves experience in its full range, we deprive ourselves of the chance to become mature and strong. We cling instead to a regressive, foetal kind of "safety" in which we are more than ever vulnerable to any disturbance of our closed world.

Thus the person "stuck" with a failed relationship remains stuck; he cannot grow beyond the failure unless he opens himself to a new experience, providing the opportunity for growth, for changed behavior and better choices. The non-driving wife who sticks close to her husband, or the woman who won't go back to school because "the children need" her, may miss forever the opening out of experience, the chance to develop into a woman who could balance and integrate the activities of a wife and mother with her own independent needs. Sometimes we fear such growth, knowing it will lead us away from familiar paths, and not knowing where, or how far, it will lead. But in fearing it we fail to realize the increases in the strength and capacities of the self which are inherent in the expansion of experience, and which enable us to cope with the conflicts occasioned by our growth.

In any case, we avoid growth only at our peril. Old wives' tales, and those of latter-day scientists, tell us that even the womb is penetrated with danger signals, physiological warnings indicating not only physical threat but also threat to the emotional ambiance of the environment, which is sensed through changes in the chemistry of the mother's body. Similarly, even a womb-like security cannot lull us into complete ignorance of what threatens us, especially since our threats come not only from the outside but also from within ourselves. Denial of the impulses of the self toward new growth places these impulses in the category of threats. In an effort to protect a status quo which is felt to be safe, we suppress those strivings which may disturb it.

A woman may say, *My husband wouldn't want me to go to work.* What does this really mean? She may be saying, *I don't want to go to work;* but she may want to avoid the responsibility for this choice. Or perhaps what she wishes is to tell others and herself that her husband is unreasonable or, on the other hand, that he cherishes her or feels a strong need for her presence in the home. She may be saying, *I don't want to go to work because I feel safer at home.* She may be saying, *I don't want to go to work, but I'm afraid it would cause trouble with my husband.* She may be saying,

I want to go to work, but I'm afraid that would make me feel like more of a person and less willing to live with my husband's limitations. The husband, on the other hand, may indeed object to his wife's working. Perhaps he fears that his needs will be neglected, or that she may grow beyond him, or that she will demand more power within the family, or even that she may meet someone else.

This is not to imply, of course, that all women should, or should want to, work outside the home, or that we need not consider the responses of our mates in making such choices. It is rather to suggest that we can have various motives for making or avoiding changes in our lives; and that many of them have to do with the sense of safety or danger. When we close off the possibility of change or of new kinds of experience, and especially when we make pat explanations to ourselves—particularly those laying the responsibility on someone else—then we are covering over feelings that it may be vital to open up and explore.

When such feelings are suppressed, they continue to press for a hearing, and may take on less positive forms. The woman who feels her husband restrains her growth may become hostile toward him without saying or knowing why. The man who hates his work, but is afraid to think of changing it because of his family responsibilities, may become bad-tempered with his wife or begin to spend his time away from home.

THE "SAFETY" OF DEFENSES

All of us have feelings that we are afraid to bring into the light of our own recognition. The anger we harbor toward someone close, when we seem to be helpless and constrained, may be hidden even from ourselves. Hostility carried within ourselves from childhood is even more likely to be hidden and feared. Our feelings of dependence and vulnerability—that we are small, weak, fragile, insecure, in need of someone's love—may also be feelings we wish to hide and forget, for they remind us of the tenuousness of our safety.

For each of us there are things we would rather not know, would rather not think, would rather not feel, would rather not remember, because they remind us of conflicts and dangers in our inner or outer world. Whether real or imagined, they are threats to our maintenance of safe, inviolate, conflict-free space, both in our immediate world and within ourselves.

We can think of the human psyche, like the human body, as always striving to maintain its homeostasis, its dynamic balance. The psyche or self, like the body, must continually satisfy its needs, using whatever resources are available. Like the body, the psyche must also muster its resources to combat stress and hazard, and it must be ever alert to signals of danger.

We all receive warning signals of threats to our safety or our psychic comfort. Some of these signals are conscious, others are subliminal. Some have to do with threats which are distant in their sources and global in their extent, such as the threat of nuclear or biochemical warfare or of chemical contamination of our food. Some threats are tangible and potentially major, such as violence in Vietnam or in Detroit; yet they remain distant because they do not happen to involve us personally. Illness, accidents, crime in the streets, the death of a beloved person: All are major threats which remain, for most of us, most of the time, merely potential disasters, not necessarily consciously feared or dreaded, until, upon occasion, they take on a shocking reality—either in our own life or in the life of someone we know.

Although illness, violence, and death are physical threats when they take their immediate form, they are also psychic threats, whether immediate or remote: They cause in us a constant, low-level anxiety which is one of the internal stresses our psyche has to combat. Added to this chronic stress may be others which are more specific—certain health problems or family problems which are a part of our reality at any given time.

We have to live with these realistic dangers somehow, remaining alert in order to deal with them, yet not allowing ourselves to be overwhelmed with anxiety. We also have to live with our own feelings—about problems, about people, about ourselves—and with our own hidden, unacceptable impulses and urges and the anxiety they provoke.

Anxiety is our psychic early warning system. Depending on the nature and immediacy of problems and problem-feelings, its signals can be subdued or more intense—a discreet buzzer, a constant fifty-cycle hum that seems merely a background to other signals, or a persistent, nudging bell. Sometimes problems cease to be merely problems; they become louder than life and overwhelm our emotional sound system. People become persecutors, setting off a static that blocks any other signal. Our own feelings become monsters, set loose, unbounded, triggering a wild, clanging alarm in the house of the self.

To keep these warnings in check and at a reasonable level, we employ defenses. Defenses are our manipulations of perception and thinking, designed to maintain our feeling of safety even in the face of events seen as problems, people seen as persecutors, or thoughts and feelings felt as monstrous in ourselves.

Our most primitive defense is called *denial.* Denial is the attempt to do away with something perceived as threatening simply by denying its existence. We call this defense primitive because its source lies at an early stage of personality development as well as of societal development. Denial operates at the level of magic, where the world or the wish is the deed, before the ego has fully gathered its powers to test reality and to cope with the threats and problems reality presents.

We see denial in the magical thinking of children from a very early age. The mother leaves; the toddler, feeling her absence, shakes her head and says *Mommy no go bye-bye.* Even earlier, the infant, bombarded by stimuli that are too chaotic and too intense, lapses into a somnolent state that is his only recourse.

Denial is what we do when we can't stand a feeling or a complex of feelings. Denial and repression are ways of saying *No* to urges and experiences we can't handle with the other resources of the self. Repression refers to the internal warding off of impulses or drives within the self; the unacceptable need or wish is warded off or kept out of consciousness. Denial, or the denial defense, refers to our perceptions of the world, of other people, and of the self; it means denying what we see, what we feel, what we experience.

The use of denial is not confined to children's thinking. Even in our adult selves, early modes of defense coexist with our more elaborate defenses. We all know people who "can't hear" criticism, or who "look the other way" when presented with a problem. Procrastination is a form of denial; in putting off a task, we deny the necessity of doing it.

In denial and repression, thoughts and feeings that are frightening or conflict-ridden are avoided. Needs that do not seem possible to fulfill are treated as if they do not exist. Everything which threatens the existing order of the personality and the person's life style, self-concept, and network of relationships is felt as a threat and so denied. A woman says of her husband, *I can't be angry with him; I can't allow myself to get angry, because if I do then I could never get back to the way it was.* A man wears a "shit-eating grin" as he tells all the hurtful things his wife does toward him. The pain, the affect that goes with the words, is denied.

Denial and repression turn off feelings a person can't bear to encounter. The person tries to negate intolerable fear, unbearable pain, unbounded rage. A child whose mother is hospitalized for a long period may cover his feelings, pretending not to care, not to feel the terrible sense of abandonment. Denial says, *I don't care. It doesn't matter.* Denial "laughs off" pain and rage. Denial shows the person's fear of her own feelings and of what others offer to the self. Denial says, *I am not important; This is not important; Feelings are not important;* and *Nothing can be done about it anyway.*

A man working two jobs is asked, "Don't you feel you need to take time for yourself?" He answers, *No, I do everything for my family.* "What are you doing for yourself?" *Nothing.* "How about going out to dinner this weekend?" *I don't need that kind of stuff.* The answer is *No; Can't; Don't; Nothing; Never.* The needs of the self are denied. In this denial, the person is seeking safety. *I don't care what happens to me, and this isn't real anyway* means, or seems to mean, that nothing can really threaten the self.

In reality, this "safety" through denial leaves us helpless and more seriously endangered. We cannot muster our forces against a threat we refuse to recognize, nor can we meet needs we refuse even to perceive. Cultures, governments, social groups of all kinds, families, couples, and individual personalities have disintegrated because of their failure to gather their resources to meet new needs, the needs of change. When the "safety" of denial is the predominant value, what could be an opportunity becomes an occasion for avoidance. The denied feelings are locked away and denied their function as signals for change and growth; instead they fester within the self. The integrity and vitality of the organism are sacrificed in order to maintain the defense. Growing space is given up; opportunity is lost; energy is drained off perpetually, increasingly, in the effort to shore up a rigid, restricting structure.

This is not to say that denial cannot be healthy and perform a vital function, especially in its usual, partial forms. For example, denial is normal as an early stage of reaction to a severe loss, such as the death of a loved person, or to the anticipation of a loss that seems intolerable. Denial, then, in the desperation of the moment, offers a sanctuary for the disintegrating self. Then, as the self gathers its strength, the ban on realistic perception is lifted—partially, gradually, intermittently. This in turn must give way to a full recognition of the loss, and the appropriate response in feeling, however painful. Denial can offer only a temporary, partial safety; it must be given up in order for an experience to be worked through and mastered. That is why someone who has not mourned a loss fully and with eventual acceptance may become depressed long after the fact; the feeling, never dealt with and laid to rest, remains to haunt the house of the self.

The same is true of the chronic denial which is one of our ways of dealing with chronic hazard, such as the threat of nuclear war or the reality of our own eventual death. We cannot be truly safe within ourselves by denying these realities; yet we cannot live with them in the forefront of consciousness. Against these threats we employ, with other defenses, a partial and very pervasive denial; but we are most secure if we can venture, from time to time, into the thought of these possibilities and the feelings they produce, so that they are not always lingering in the wings, always shadowing the periphery of our consciousness.

It is most important to remember that defenses are not "bad," even though we tend to think of them in their negative, restrictive, compulsive forms. In fact, defenses are vital to our sanity. Without some ordering of perception, the senses and the brain would be overwhelmed with messages; without some filtering of experience, the ego would be incapacitated, flooded with feeling. Defenses operate to preserve the ego against its own impulses and against attack, loss, and rejection—even against acceptance that is confused with over-closeness, with merging and consequent loss of the self.

We all have crazy thoughts and crazy feelings. For most of us, most of the time, these are "bound" within an integrated personality, locked in the basement of the house of the self, or entertained in the living space in carefully limited and channeled forms. When we see a person in a psychotic episode, we can see how we might be without our defenses. Anyone feels, for example, a tinge of mistrust in meeting a new person, and this feeling is self-protective; but a meeting can also inspire a positive feeling, a wish to like and to trust and to share with the other person. This is a normal ambivalence, and the particular blend of trust and mistrust varies from one personality to another. But for a person in psychosis the feelings may be undiluted; this person may literally recoil in fear, or rush to embrace the stranger.

Our defenses protect us from knowing our thoughts and feelings in their naked, extreme forms. They help us to keep our stresses at tolerable levels. When they are flexible and adaptive, they can be called strategies; they operate with intelligence, to help us utilize our resources. It is only when defenses become rigid and automatic that they are maladaptive, and then they severely limit our experiential world. Then they are another womb, holding us seemingly "safe" but confined, constricted, unable to grow and become strong within ourselves.

THE "SAFETY" OF ADDICTIONS

The person who feels empty can't feel safe. Ideally, when we leave the mother and grow to be ourselves, we gradually learn to fill the self and to get—through our own efforts and our own giving—good, nourishing food for the self from others. This means, of course, not only the food that fills our bodies, but the emotional and mental "food" that we need for full satisfaction as human beings: knowledge, attention, stimulation, affection, loving commitment, good feelings, and good experience. Without learning to give this kind of nourishment to ourselves, and to engage in relationships that allow us to receive from others, we cannot develop into secure, independent selves.

But of course we are not born with these capacities, and their development depends on the original "feeding," in every sense, by the mother and other parenting figures; and similarly, this development depends upon being fed, through the long process of growth, in ways appropriate to our age and level of maturity. At first, the infant remains close to the breast, wholly dependent on its rhythmic return for his food, and on the repeated experience of being filled for his sense of safety. Then, gradually, through many stages of growth, the child learns that it is safe to grow away from the source of food and comfort; that he can learn to feed himself and then to obtain his own food; that there are sources outside the family for comfort and fulfillment; and that to leave the mother need not mean emptiness and hunger. Ideally, the adult who emerges from the growth process of the child is someone who feels secure about the fulfillment of her needs, and about her own giving and receiving in relationships with others.

But the world is full of people who have not been this fortunate in growth. Very few of us feel totally secure about being "fed." Very few of us have been fed so reliably, and in ways so suited to our own rhythms of need and of growth, that we feel fully able to find our food in the world, and to give and receive in our relations with others in fully satisfying ways.

No one can give while feeling the self to be empty and poor. The person who emerges from childhood uncertain of being well fed cannot feel safe and free in giving to others. We give from fullness, not from short rations. The person who has not felt reliably fed remains preoccupied with his own hunger; he feels giving as an emptying of the self, and lacks the confidence that if he gives, he will also receive and be filled again.

We are talking here not only of physical hunger, or even of the more obvious emotional deprivations a child can suffer in growing—although physical hunger and emotional starvation are of course the most serious sources of feelings of emptiness. For most of us, deprivation has been partial and subtle, and affects us only partially and in ways that don't totally destroy our capacity to have relationships. Yet the effects of these early, unsatisfied hungers are pervasive, persistent, and real.

We need to remember here that we are not talking simply of a self that happens to be empty, a strong shell without adequate contents. It is only with good emotional nourishment that we are able to build a self at all, just as the body develops only with the help of good food. As physical deprivation at certain stages of growth produces effects impossible to reverse, so emotional deprivation produces a psychic structure that is vulnerable and frail. In order to give and receive in satisfying ways, we need to build a self that can contain good, that can build up resources over time from which to give to others, and that can take in what others can give and use it for the self.

THE "SAFETY" OF ADDICTIONS

We are touching here on the problem of insecure giving and receiving because this encourages restriction, fixation, and addiction, in which many people in our society seek their safety. By addiction we do not mean only the specific physiological dependency on drugs or alcohol that has done mortal damage on a grand scale to individuals, families, and the whole urban society, although these forms of addiction are the most overt in their destructive power. There are nine million alcoholics in this country alone, and millions of people addicted to cigarettes, pills, star images, ideas, and wishes for motorcycles. But these are only the most easily identified of those people who seek safety in addiction. Our television commercials and our groups formed to wean people from smoking or overeating are eloquent testimony to the numbers who try to fill up the empty place in themselves with food, or to take security from sucking on a cigarette.

Addiction is essentially a repetitive, compulsive effort to find, in the satisfaction of a part of the self, the security and fulfillment of the whole self. Of course this effort is doomed to failure. The transient satisfaction of one process—smoking, drinking, eating, having sex—cannot be internalized, it can only be repeated, so that the adult self remains chained to its addiction, forever trying to squeeze satisfaction from the breast of a partial reality, and forever finding there only a bitter mockery of mother's milk.

The person who has not received enough as a child can't give as an adult. And since he can't give to others in adult relationships, he can't receive even the fulfillment of his present needs, let alone fill up the empty place left by earlier hungers. The person tries desperately to fill the empty place by taking in candy, extra food, cigarettes, drugs, liquor, TV, books, designer clothing, money, power tools, prestige automobiles, chemical "highs." Parts of the self are fed; the rest of the self grows hungry. The products and functions of certain parts of the self are given—talk from the mouth, thoughts from the head, work from the muscles, sex from the genitals—but the whole self is not given to others or involved with others. And the relations with others which could offer, over time, a real, internal satisfaction are fragmented and broken; the real resources of the self are scattered by a self not strong enough to contain them.

This is the real and damaging meaning of addiction, whether the addiction is to food, drink, drugs, ideas, processes, or even to a relationship of dependency on a "love object." It is an habitual, repetitive, compulsive constriction of the process of giving and receiving with other human beings. The addict is trapped in a world of objects, trapped in a process which tries to substitute a part for the wholeness of others and the self. The addiction can never do away with the hunger, which can be filled only in the development of the full self. The addiction can never provide safety, but only the danger, both repetitive and chronic, of the ultimate starvation of the self.

THE SAFETY OF LIMITS

What does a person really need to be safe? Since bodily experience underlies all psychic experience, we can think of this in a biological model. First of all, we need "food" for our bodies and our selves. This means the literal food that keeps our bodies alive. It also means, in this context, everything we take in, everything good that we receive—information, stimulation, affection, good feelings, good experience. We need to take in, we need to receive, and the capacity to receive good and utilize it for growth is basic both to our real, physical survival and to our emotional safety.

In order to receive and to take in good, we have to give and to discriminate, to express and to expel, to get rid of our wastes and our "bad" thoughts and feelings, as well as to give forth our creative products. This means we have to have avenues of expression, ways to move our bodies and our feelings, and places where it is safe to "let go" with whatever we have inside us—good, bad, knowledge, confusion, shit, sorrow, rage, love.

What makes it safe to take in good food, and express the contents of the self? Basically, the knowledge that we can set limits, both on what we take in and on what we let go. The safe-feeling self can take in food in answer to its own body rhythms, without starving or gorging; the self-feeling self is free to feed in response to hunger and to stop when the hunger is satisfied.

The safe-feeling self is not a deprived, voracious infant living in fear of devouring the mother and the magic breast; nor is this self a clinging, desperately dependent person who drains others of their resources; nor is the one who dares not take anything from others, for fear of letting loose in the self the monstrous wish to feed without limit. The safe-feeling self is not an addict, seeking in a single, compulsive mode of instant gratification the return of the magic breast. The safe-feeling self can differentiate among kinds of "food" and their uses and sources without confusing food with love, drunken conviviality with fellowship, sex with affection, or compulsive activity with good experience—and so repetitively pushing the same hopeless button like a rat misled in a maze. The safe-feeling self can take in good food without fearing it is poisoned or will cause indigestion, and yet it can limit what is taken, and when, and how. The safe-feeling self can take in good food and good experience regulated by a personal map and an inner clock.

The same sense of safety through limits offers the freedom of "letting go" of the contents of the self. The self-feeling self can give up its wastes, again in accord with the rhythms of the body, making room for more food or more input into the self. The self-feeling self can vent anger without merely "dumping," placing it where it belongs and expressing the needs of the self without altogether losing control. Since the anger is both limited and expressed, it does not become a monster of rage let loose in the house of the self, and there is no need to fear its murderous force.

The self-feeling self can assert facts and feelings without fearing they will do damage or cause shame to the self. The self-feeling self can give forth its creative products without diminishing them or confusing them with shit, but keeping a sense of their value. The safe-feeling self can give, within limits, without giving away everything and therefore without the fear of being left empty and starving. The safe-feeling self knows that what is voided will be replaced, that what is given to others will have its balance with what is received. The safe-feeling self can give up bad experience to make way for good, and can give up some—but not all—of the familiar to make way for the new.

Taking in and letting go, giving and receiving, are continual dynamic processes in our lives, a constant interchange with others and with our physical world. Our only true "safety" is a safety in this dynamic sense, the safety of flexibility and movement, residing in a self which is felt as stable but not rigid, able to create structure and limits, yet not imprisoned within them. The safety is a feeling of being safe to *be,* to *do,* to *think,* to *feel,* to have experience, and to obtain and expand with this experience. Truly safe space is not a womb but an expanding universe, both within and outside the self.

This is still not all of what we require. With all our giving and receiving, we also need more intimate forms of safe space and safe time: time that is free of intrusion and demands; space—physical, psychic, and social—that is wholly our own. We all need doors we can lock and open by our own choice. We need times and places to rest, to retreat, to restore ourselves. And we need the rhythmic return of familiar faces, people we count upon and trust, people who do not invade our private space, yet who are with us as trusted companions.

THE SAFE HOUSE OF THE SELF

We can think of the self, then, as a special kind of house. It has a secure foundation, unshaken by storms or by invaders. It has protective walls, defining, structuring, and enclosing space for use for the purposes of the self. The walls are made of a flexible, permeable membrane that lets in good experience and helps to screen out bad; this allows the house to breathe through its pores, and to expand or contract as the weather requires. The safe house has a good thermostat, regulating its own internal climate, whatever the season. It has ample windows to let in the sun and the air, and shutters to close out the cold; and it has a big yard, its interface with the world.

The safe house of the self has doors to admit visitors, and room for certain of these to remain through many seasons. It has good figures installed in the kitchen, offering a source of nourishment and comfort within the self; and it has protectors, also securely installed, to turn away enemies at the door. It has storage space—but it is not cluttered with unusable inheritances from the past.

The safe house of the self has a work room with a good, strong light, where thoughts, projects, and events can be examined and seen clearly, and where mirrors offer a true reflection. It has enough space to wrestle, to thrash, and to play, without fear of any damage that could not be repaired. And it has a private room, a place to linger for love, for rest, for the reverie that invites dreams and secret hopes, wishes and memories—the innumerable mysteries of the self.

Unsafe Space: Nightmare, Childhood, and Psychosis

TWO

> There was a monster under the bed, and I couldn't move.
>
> I can't remember anything that happened before I was ten years old.
>
> Everybody lives in fantasy. But fantasy became his reality.

The house of the unsafe self is a haunted house, a Bluebeard's castle with many barred doors and forbidden rooms, and monsters roaming the hallways. The foundations are shaky, so the house groans in the winds of change. The walls are easy knockdowns, like a stage setting. The internal weather is uncertain. There is great danger of running out of food. The rooms are littered, the passageways blocked with garbage; the windows are grimy and can't let in the sun. Each visitor is a potential enemy, and enemies can walk right into the house. The yard outside is a minefield.

What makes these psychic spaces so unsafe? The person whose self is this chronically unsafe house, as well as the person in an acute state of fright, is showing in severe forms the fears we all carry within ourselves. No matter how secure our sense of self or how advanced our concept of safety, our bodies remain fragile, our psyches remain vulnerable to stress, our environment remains hazardous, and our existence remains contingent on many accidental factors. Psychic safety, let alone fulfillment, lies in a perpetually shifting balance of forces, like a buoy that is anchored but afloat in choppy waters. Psychic survival depends on the security of the anchors, the buoyancy and resilience of the personality, and finally on the external weather.

What are the fears that can drown or invade the self? We know them most vividly in fantasy, in nightmares, in the fears of childhood and in the terrors of psychosis. In these states of consciousness, our wishes and fears have free play and unbounded power. In these processes, the structuring, limiting, realistic self does not prevail. Our wishes and longings predominate, and with them—sometimes identical with them—our fears.

THE UNSAFE SPACE OF NIGHTMARES

In dreams and in fantasy, and most of all in nightmares, our feelings are made graphic, dramatized in their most extreme forms. Our longings, our fears, our rages become wild beasts, vampires, rampaging monsters, unbound and swollen beyond our human size and strength. In nightmares we chase and are chased, we flee for our lives, we do murder ourselves. In nightmares we suffer fully the horror of being lost, of familiar faces turning strange, of anxiety that invades us from an unknown source.

People who have nightmares are afraid to fall asleep. They are afraid to find themselves trapped again in a nightmare world, flooded with nightmare feelings, unable to breathe, in a cold sweat, their pulses pounding. Sometimes the dread, guilt, or panic of the nightmare persists until the person gets out of bed, walks around the room, and restores in himself the sense of being in a safe place.

Nightmares are most frequent in young children; and they have common motifs which include the fear of being abandoned, the fear of being bitten, the fear of being chased by monsters, and the fear of being devoured. The young child, waking from such a nightmare in a dark room, may streak out of bed, screaming, seeing the nightmare monster still there in the darkness. For children, the sleeping and the waking world are close together, since both are heavily infused with fantasy.

Nightmares tend to subside as we grow older, but they surge up again at certain stages in our lives. There is some evidence that old nightmares may return and that new ones may emerge at critical developmental phases. These may occur when a child is sent away to camp, when an adolescent graduates from high school, or when a parent dies. Such phases may also occur at less defined, more dynamically determined turning points in a person's life when, just as in childhood, there are very great strains and stresses on the capacity to handle one's feelings and to take in and to structure perceived reality that is new, strange, and in some ways threatening to the sense of safety.

A great part of the terror of and within nightmares comes from the furiously intense emotion they generate and express. In daily life, with a fully functioning daytime ego, we are guarded to some degree against the full force of our emotions. Our fears and our wishes are very much mitigated by a sense of reality that, generally speaking, limits their expression.

But reality does not govern the world of nightmare. In the nightmare, our worst fears and our "worst" wishes come true. The nightmare, or night horse, is a terrifying monster of irresistible power; it sweeps us away into a world that has few or none of the landmarks of safety. From the viewpoint of the nightmare, our waking life is itself a dream of safety; and we are pinned in *this* moment, *this* reality in which threat and terror have overrun their bounds, and we have lost our usual powers to limit or outrun them. In the compelling world of the nightmare, we are caught in the inescapable grip of the nightmare feeling, by which we mean the overwhelming sense of *something extraordinarily wrong,* of being unable to exercise our daytime forces to meet threats of normal dimensions.

In a nightmare of being chased, the nightmare feeling is one of being unable to run away, or unable to run fast enough, or unable to move at all. In a nightmare of wrestling with a demon, the nightmare feeling is one of being overpowered, or not being strong enough, or having no power to move or to resist. In a nightmare of hiding from a murderer, the nightmare feeling is one of inevitably being found and killed. In a nightmare of having done murder oneself, the nightmare feeling is one of inevitably being discovered, being revealed, being found out, being unable to hide what one is and what one has done.

In some nightmares, the feelings of horror, guilt, and dread are peculiarly absent. Appalling events and grotesque images are treated calmly, with only a vague sense of *something wrong;* but the feelings follow us in waking, like a poisonous aftertaste. Sometimes a familiar scene is punctuated by one grotesque element. There is a sense of profound distortion, of dissonance, of surreality. Our normal experience is twisted and skewed, as if we had entered a universe of uncanny space, all the more terrifying because it appears familiar.

> In the dream, my mother passed my bed. I started to greet her, but suddenly realized in terror that she is dead and shouldn't be there.
>
> In the dream, I was in my house, but nothing was in the right place. There was a party, but everyone had gone home except one guest. Then I realized that person had stayed behind in order to kill me.

These are nightmares, not of monsters, but of witches and devils, of an ominous suspension of reality, a half-light in which our preposterous fears and wishes are magically made real.

The kinds of things that happen in nightmares are often portrayed in surrealistic films and art, in murder mysteries, and in science fiction. These are safe spaces for our nightmare fantasies and feelings; our experiencing of them is a freely chosen, readily controlled, inherently limited way of working through the fears expressed in fantasy and nightmare. In the safe space offered by these forms of fantasy, we can always stop reading or look away from the screen; we can approach the realm of terror vicariously, with people around us, or under conditions we ourselves control.

Ordinary dreams, too, are a safe space, in which some of the wishes, thoughts, and apprehensions we keep in the background of our waking consciousness can be given expression and play. But dreams, although in a sense freer than our waking life, are still limited by our sense of reality. Our ordinary dreams are discreet and euphemistic; they reveal our wishes, but in an indirect, symbolic, coded form. Our ordinary dreams may inspire and express anxiety, but they do not release this anxiety to such a level that we are plunged into panic, as in the nightmare.

In a nightmare, the feelings of rage, terror, guilt, dread, and overwhelming need press us too strongly to be contained in sleep. They create terrible danger even in the safe space of dreams, and send us screaming into our apparent refuge: the waking life—with its familiar, more rational structure and limits.

But the most vital aspect of our nightmares lies precisely here, in their relationship to our waking life. Nightmares are not alien to our psyches; they are an intimate form of expression of the primitive needs and fears of the self. They do not end with our waking. Rather, the monsters and nightmare figures continue to lurk in the shadows of the psyche, contained and kept in check by the energies of the waking self, which are devoted to maintaining control and a sense of reality. Despite this restraint, the nightmare figures and feelings continue to threaten and press upon the waking self.

Our nightmares are like skeletons in the psychic closet; they represent secret struggles and strivings, secret fears, wishes, and imagined deeds. The nightmare may be quickly forgotten or, like the monsters that linger in the child's dark room, it may haunt our consciousness throughout the day. In either case, the signals and feelings that spring from the sources of nightmare continue to move in the deepest levels of the self. If the nightmare is about falling, or being frozen, or being bitten, or being chased and killed, it continues to operate, in another form, as a fear of what will happen if one gets close to other human beings, or if one is left alone.

The nightmare can be thought of as a scenario presented by the most primitive part of the self. The nightmare comes forth when the rational controls of the self are let go in sleep, so that the primitive self is in command. The person who knows he harbors nightmares and night monsters is afraid to give up his controls, either to sleep or to any kind of emotion; he is especially afraid of losing control in aggression or sexuality. The person feels that to let go is to give up control to the primitive self, and to invite nightmares and night terrors into his waking life. In relaxation, as in sleep, the embattled ego is drained of its power to control the wild horses and monsters of impulse and terror.

THE UNSAFE SPACE OF CHILDHOOD

The child's ego, even in daylight, is frail, incomplete in its functioning, easily overwhelmed by fright and rage and by the power of fantasy. The younger the child, the more he is at the mercy of feeling and of distorted perception. Children, waking from nightmares, often continue screaming; it is hard for them to return to reality because their sense of reality is confused and shaky. The monster in the dream is felt to be *there,* in the closet, in the darkness. The possible and the impossible are not yet clearly distinguished.

Children only gradually, and never completely, clear their thoughts of fantasy. Even more than adults, they entertain "impossible" hopes and fears, and believe their wishes can have magical effects for good or ill. They often need to be reassured that their angry wishes do not really do the damage that is half-desired, half-feared—that, for example, to wish their parents dead is not really to kill them. They need help in learning that there are limits to the power of fantasy, boundaries to the realm of nightmare. For in a child's world, *anything can happen.*

Although we tend to think of the child's world as safe and protected, even well-tended children always live, to a degree, in unsafe space, subject to the wills of other people and to the intensity of their own strivings and emotions. The child is weak and helpless; adults are powerful. The child is flooded with emotions; adults claim rationality, set limits, and at times they coerce and punish. The child entertains fantasy; adults insist upon "reality"—and, at times, upon the projection of their own fantasy world.

Children have trouble learning perspective and proportion. The limits adults assert on thought, feeling, and behavior come hard to them. By contrast to these adult expectations and these "realistic" limits, children often feel like monsters. Like people in psychotic states of mind, they often sojourn "where the wild things are," in the realm of untrammeled fears, longings, and wishes. And, being subject to the actions, pressures, threats, powers, and whims of adults, they often fantasize and fear monsters, which are the projections of their own rage and fright, and of the feelings they experience or imagine in these oversized, powerful adults.

Children are much involved with issues of power; their magical thinking seems to invest them with enormous power, which, when combined with intense feeling, makes them monsters in their own eyes. On the other hand, they feel powerless, knowing that they are in fact small, frail, and subject to the wills and dispositions of their parents.

The extreme form of these two antithetical, yet coexistent feelings—of being power*less* and power*ful*—is what is called infantile omnipotence. We believe that the infant makes, at first, no differentiation between the self and the mothering figure or the magical, feeding breast. We believe, that, even as he begins to differentiate and to feel himself as separate, the infant feels that the mothering figure with the feeding breast comes and goes not only in response to his wishes, but by virtue of his magical power to put those wishes into effect. In other words, though powerless, he feels omnipotent. And, when this power fails and the infant is frustrated, he rages with the rage of a god or a demon.

This sense of magical omnipotence is carried into childhood, as if it were compensation for the child's actual frailty and dependence, for his relative lack of power. Only gradually, and to a degree painfully, do we give up this magical thinking and accommodate ourselves to a more realistic view of our powers to act, to think, and to feel. Perhaps the magic is given up only as we are able to replace it with a realistic capacity to take action and to make choices, so that we no longer feel totally at the mercy of the alien forces and the unfathomable wishes of others.

While we still live, to a degree, in the world of magic, we also live in the world of nightmare. For it is the condition of nightmare, as it is of the waking fantasy world of magical thinking, that we do not know ordinary limits to our own powers and those of others. In the world of no limits, anything can happen. In the world of no limits, we can have our every wish. Our rage can kill others, and the vengeful rage of others can kill us. In that world of magic and of nightmare, mere wishes have the power that our acts in reality cannot achieve.

Many folk tales and dramatic themes are based on the folly and hazard involved in using magic to put our wishes into effect. From the tale of the fisherman's wife to Faust's bargaining with the Devil, we are instructed repeatedly that we employ magic, and that we seek the outrageously unbounded gratification of our wishes only at our peril or at enormous cost. Magic is not profitable to the self. The unwise or greedy wish, or the wish that is carelessly expressed, or the ill-advised bargain which attempts to transcend the realistic limits of our existence, comes back on the protagonist, inspiring a deadly remorse. Like the hero or heroine of such tales, the child, too, senses that some of his wishes, if fully granted, could destroy his world.

It is vital to understand here that our fears reflect our wishes and longings; that is the basic ambivalence of our experience. We wish for power that would be terrifying to exercise. We have wishes that would lay waste to our whole lives. If this is true of our immediate wishes, it is equally so of our more basic desires; even these are contrary, ambivalent. We want to break out of the womb, yet we wish to remain inside; we seek a return to that rapturous comfort, yet we fear suffocation in that dark hole: We speak of "smother love." Much later, as adolescents, we fight off the embrace of the family all the more fiercely because we long to remain in its sheltering grasp. The fear is in proportion to the wish—in a sense, the fear *is* the wish—and the striving to break the bonds is in proportion to the binding force.

In the world of magic and nightmare, children are frightened by the unbounded power of wishes and by their just punishment, which is both ethically and dramatically inescapable. The psychic world of the child seems very close to the sense of reality in pre-scientific societies, where natural forces are seen as magical and certain individuals are seen as having magical powers. In primitive terms, the projected reality is that one must sacrifice to the gods, that one must observe their power and respect their limits, or else suffer their punishment.

In the child's world, parents have such superhuman powers. Because of this, and because of the child's limited power to perceive clearly and to integrate perceptions of an object, parents in this sense are fantasy figures. Infants are not born being able to perceive objects as adults perceive them. Their perceptual apparatus offers them images that are shifting and scrambled. The infant only gradually becomes able to visualize whole objects or whole figures; only little by little does he begin to recognize that these figures go away and return, and that they have safely predictable patterns of behavior toward the infant or child and toward each other. In the beginning, the child's world is full of bewilderment, uncertainty, apprehension, and confusion, mitigated only by the structuring and nurturing of the parent figures, who are seen as all-knowing and all-powerful.

Fantasy organizes perception, and lack of experience is a breeding ground for terror. Many nightmares seem to have their roots in a confused, monster-like perception that a child has about the human body and about the interaction of mother and father. Children may fantasize being trapped inside the mother's body. They may fantasize feeding, urination, and excretion as hostile interactions between themselves and their parents. They may fantasize sexuality as a cannibalistic rite, a devouring attack in which the parental figures, and potentially the child himself, are chewed up, devoured, poisoned, overpowered, destroyed. They may incestuously fantasize getting into mother for refuge and gratification, and being attacked by a revengeful father or by two monster-like figures—not in the forms of mother and father as the real, whole parents, but rather by their partialized, distorted images.

Such fantasies sound strange to us as adults, because we have covered over that early, primitive fantasy life with our elaborate and necessary structure of defenses, and because we have achieved, through growth and through the development of our ego functions, the capacity to sort out and clarify our perceptions of others. Adults in psychosis, or under severe stress, or in their nightmares, may suffer regression to such fantasies, which sound less strange to us when we hear an adult saying to a child, *I could eat you up!* or *What a delicious baby!*

Again, our psychic experience is grounded in the body, and this bodily experience, which is expressed in our language, strongly colors our perception at any given time of life. Children in particular live partially in a prehistoric landscape, in the presence of monsters we remember only in nightmare and fantasy. In that ancient landscape, parenting figures themselves are sometimes seen as monstrous or superhuman: They cut and chop each other with their voices; they penetrate with their glances; they devour with their hungry, insistent demands for love and obeisance; they bathe the child with the sun of their love or leave a wasteland behind their absence.

The child, in successive stages of development, sucks, bites, excretes, withholds, and feels that this is what people are doing to each other and to him in many other forms. Again, this sounds less strange to us when we hear an adult say, *He fed me one thing; she fed me another; I was fed up!* The child in the oral stage, in constant motion, putting everything in his mouth at the same moment that he sees it, knows little of the difference between perceiving and devouring. He "knows" an object by trying to eat it, just as a man, in the much later genital stage of development, was once said to "know" a woman by getting into her sexually. The child in the anal stage expels his feces as gifts of love or as outbursts of aggression, or he withholds them as desperate, defiant assertions of self. Children, imagining sexual relations and wondering where children really come from, often develop fantasies in which sex is confused with eating and excreting; they may think that a baby grows in the mother's stomach from something she eats, and is expelled like feces. Adult men and women, in the full range of sexual behavior, may suck and bite each other as well as penetrate; we are genital, anal, and oral in the context of a single act. We act and perceive even as adults, and far more so as children, on many developmental levels, and, accordingly, with a large admixture of fantasy. Until it is clarified, the body is a fantasy body.

How, then, is a child to understand clearly the involvement of his mother and father? They are, or seem to be, at each other, into each other, with each other; together they make "the beast with two backs"—the two monsters are made one in copulation, at the sight of which the child, half awake and bewildered, stands rooted in terror. That is the primal scene in the original version to which Freud introduced us. But the vision of the primal scene that the child has to take in and integrate is even more stunning and much more comprehensive. It is "the scene" in a more colloquial sense—the entire interaction of mother and father, with each other and with the child. Our bodily fantasies, like our bodily experience, are not divorced from the thinking and doing of the rational self. As adults, we can separate these fantasies from reality in our thoughts, and clarify them for our understanding and our sanity. But our experience, in its real, living flow, remains continuous. The body of fantasy and the body of reality lie down together in the bed of the self; and their actions are mingled there to make the variegated, multicolored, enriched, and sometimes poisoned whole that is our total experience of ourselves and of each other. The enormous task of childhood is the blending, channeling, and integration of these forces to make a self that can see, feel, and move in the world. That is the task of structuring and of construction by which we make paths through the unsafe space of childhood, domesticate its monsters, and set limits to fear and to the magical powers of wishes.

THE UNSAFE SPACE OF PSYCHOSIS

We live, as children and in nightmare, in the realm of "wild things," among monsters, demons, and grotesque happenings. That is also where, in psychotic states of mind, we may return and remain as prisoners. To people who are psychotic, and to many who are merely severely anxious, much of daily experience has the quality of nightmare. For such people the fabric of daily life itself is unsafe; it is a ghost-garment obscuring the clarity of what is real, a floating veil suggestive of unseen dangers and hidden motives. Everything is distorted by this veil, and human faces cannot shine through it. Overwhelming feelings and overwhelming fears chronically distort perception of the self and of others.

Powerful feelings do not belong only to psychotic states. The primitive idea of demons or of possession by spirits is close to the sense that many of us sometimes have of our feelings; as though they are not native but alien to ourselves, as though their sources were not within us but in another person or in some unknown field of fources. It is as if we are invaded by a fright that cripples our being, by a rage that overwhelms our rationality. At such times, feelings take on a mysterious power that threatens our usual control. The person asks, *Why do I feel this way?* or *Why is this happening to me?* but he arrives at no answer. The source of the feelings itself is clouded with fear.

A woman says, *I feel under a terrible pressure and I don't know why. I have moods I don't understand, and they frighten me. I fly off the handle at every little thing. I'm afraid I'm driving my husband away. I'm afraid I'm losing my mind.* This woman is probably not psychotic, but she is having nightmare feelings; she is hiding their sources from herself, and she has the sense of going out of control. Her inner space has become unsafe, and her rage and the fright it both covers and inspires are making her interactional space unsafe as well. She is not delusional; she knows, realistically, that her feelings originate in herself. Yet she sometimes *feels as if* she were inhabited by a demon or an evil spirit, so estranged is she from the hidden sources of her own feelings.

When we ask this woman, "Are you eating well?" she replies, *I only eat because I must.* When we ask, "Are you sleeping at night?" she says, *No, I have trouble going to sleep, and then I wake many times during the night. I have bad dreams.* Even her bodily rhythms are upset: She cannot take food in any gratifying sense; she cannot take pleasure in sexuality; she cannot rest, for monsters invade her sleep. Even her bodily functions have become alien and somehow frightening, set awry by the nameless, faceless, monstrous forces which seem to have taken over her being.

Is this woman "crazy?" Probably not, so long as she continues to understand that what is amiss lies within herself, and does not come to believe she is literally possessed by demons, or that the monsters that haunt her sleep are anything but dream figures, the products of her own imagination. But people often, under the pressure of overwhelming feelings of anxiety or guilt or dread, begin to fear they are "going crazy." This fear in itself makes their inner and outer space feel even more unsafe, and makes them even more afraid of learning and of revealing how they really feel.

It can help us to remember that "craziness" is not something totally alien to a "normal" state of mind, even though the sense of alienation from normal experience is profound; and yet that, on the other hand, being "crazy" is definably different from being sane. In psychosis—as in nightmare or in the child's episode of raging—a person may live awhile "where the wild things are." When this happens, it means the same thing as in nightmare or in the child's tantrum—that *the sense of reality is lost.* Having a sense of reality means that a person knows limits, knows proportion, knows the difference between reality and fantasy, and is able to perceive what is real and distinguish it from what is imagined. The sense of reality involves a capacity to shape and to test our own perceptions, and to set limits upon the distorting power of emotion. All cultures strive to discriminate fantasy and reality.

When we are flooded with anxiety, washed with longing or apprehension, or drowned in a sense of guilt, then our perceptions become unclear. We see as if we were looking through water. Our thoughts are like a funhouse mirror, giving back a distorted perception of ourselves; the windows of our eyes are clouded as we look at others. We become monsters to ourselves; we see others as monsters or persecutors, and the whole landscape of our life space appears threatening, or denuded and barren.

In some degree, these experiences are common to many people. Some distortion of reality occurs in every person. The differences are of degree, kind, duration, and cause. When we ask ourselves, *Am I crazy?* or *Is this person crazy?*, the crucial questions are: *To what degree* is the perception of reality distorted? In what *areas*? *How much* of the life space is affected? What is the *quality* of the distortion? *How long* does it go on? How does it affect the person's *behavior*? What are the *causes* of the distortion, both the precipitating stresses and the more basic sources?

These are crucial questions because they help us to understand when to be alarmed, and how alarmed to be, about ourselves or about another person. We are right to have concern about states of feeling that trouble us, change our behavior, or interfere with our sense of safety or emotional comfort. But we can have concern and we can acknowledge stress—even overwhelming stress—and we can seek help with that stress without calling ourselves or others "crazy." Sometimes people are afraid to seek psychotherapy for the same reasons they might avoid going to a doctor, fearing to learn they have cancer or heart disease. Unless we can understand that "normal" and "crazy" states of consciousness and feeling take place on a long continuum of experience, having many gradations and fluctuations, and that these states have much in common with each other as well as having definable differences between them, we are in a difficult position from which to seek help with our stress, or even to allow ourselves to recognize that we *have* stress and troubled feelings.

There is a difference between the man who accuses his wife of serving him bad food and the man who believes his food is poisoned. There is a difference between the taxi driver who rants and raves at another driver and the one who stabs the other with a knife. There is a difference between the woman who watches television all day, too anxious either to leave the house or to experience it in silence, and the woman who stands in the corridor of a psychiatric hospital, literally too frightened to move a step in any direction unless she is led by the hand. There are differences between the mother who yells at her child to relieve her own tension, the one who hits the child, and the one who throws the child against the wall. And there are differences between the person who wishes fleetingly for the oblivion of death, the one who thinks seriously of suicide in a crisis of mourning, the person recurrently preoccupied with suicidal thoughts, the person who makes a definite plan, the one who gestures as a call for help, and the successful or near-successful suicide.

But these shades of behavior are not fixed, known entities in any person; and, while they are different in their implications, both for the person and for someone who tries to help him, they speak of the same feelings and the same fears. These gradations of behavior show the intensity of the fear or other feeling in the person at a given time, and the degree to which he is able to contain it within realistic bonds.

There is a sense, in encountering a person in a truly psychotic state of mind, that the person has "crossed a line." The "line" is the boundary of what we normally consider a sense of reality in thought, feeling, and behavior. As in physical states of health or illness, normality and craziness each cover a vast range of capacities and impairments. The person who is not psychotic may not be realistic in the strictest sense or in every respect. But the person's thoughts are not distorted to the point that he cannot function in the world, and they are not totally dominated by fantasy. The person's feelings, even though they may be quite out of proportion to a situation, are still moderated by a concept of proportion. The person's behavior is not incompatible with his or her own welfare or that of other people. The person who is saying *I have feelings that frighten me* is still locating the feelings within the self, and viewing them as cause for concern. This is different from projecting fright and rage onto others, and saying *They are out to get me;* and it is different from being so steeped in anxiety that even the self-observant ego is drowned. To live within a sense of reality that is colored, partially or from time to time, by the waking dream of fantasy is different from moving wholly into a fantasy world. To see other people as hostile is different from seeing them as conspirators and killers. To feel oneself as deprived and alone in a harsh, comfortless world is different from feeling oneself as literally starving and helpless, unable to move or to survive.

To the person in psychosis, reality itself becomes an enemy. The confusion, terror, and despair within the self are projected out onto the world, which wears the evil skin of nightmare, perhaps overlaid by the shimmering, easily rent fabric of a manic state, or the blank sheet of schizoid withdrawal. The psychotic vision of reality may be openly terrifying, with a feeling of being menaced by mysterious monsters or bizarre objects. Ordinary occurrences, everyday implements, or human faces may inspire horror; significant words may become not mere symbols of relationship and feeling, but bombs and poisoned barbs—the real embodiment of destructive wishes and of fear of destruction.

The nightmare quality of the psychotic consciousness is compounded by the fact that the perceived world, the perceiver, and the perceiving process are all discolored by terror. Such a process forms in a hostile, cold, toxic environment, where touching, looking, eating, and excreting are all felt to be perilous. The psychotic life space reproduces the original life space of childhood, a space that was felt as a desert devoid of nourishment and barren of feeling; or as a wilderness prowled by nameless wild beasts; or as a constantly shifting series of kaleidoscopic pictures, offering no permanent image or deeper dimension; or as a terrain of jagged rocks, the sharp-edged shapes of rage and hatred. We use these metaphors of feeling because it is this global damage, this pervasive discoloration of the world, that makes it impossible for the psychotic person to function in his own life space. As long as the psychotic sense of the world persists, it must be defended with all the weapons at the command of the self. The person must deny reality—by withdrawing from the reality of feeling, or from the reality of responsibility for the self, or, as in the manic state, from any perception of the terrifying darkness and threat reality seems to contain.

The person in psychosis, trying to survive as an unmanageable self in an unmanageable world, must wall out whatever he cannot tolerate in this world, and must project out into the world whatever he cannot tolerate in the self. The rage within the self may be transformed, in the psychotic imagination, into another person's intent to kill. The envious, attacking, and self-attacking eye of the self may be projected onto someone who is seen as a policeman-like figure, always watching and waiting to attack. The guilt carried within the self may become a firm belief that one has done mortal damage to someone. The feeling of utter helplessness may be, at length, transformed into the psychotic version of infantile omnipotence: the grandiose belief that one is all-powerful or is some famous or notorious figure, either in disguise or unrecognized by others. The grief of loss or the lifelong depression of never having had what one needs may be replaced by the denial of loss, or by a rosy delusion that fills, in fantasy, the empty place in the self, or by a world that feels safer because all feeling and all involvement in life are denied. The confusion, chaos, and contradictions of a psychic life space that has not allowed one to structure a secure self may be spat out again in the split, coded, and fragmented messages, the "word salad" of the schizophrenic.

In other words, the person who is trapped in psychosis, as the child is trapped in childhood and the dreamer in nightmare, lives in a chronic state of psychic emergency, using the most extreme and desperate measures that seem to offer a chance for survival—even attack on the self, even fragmenting of a perception by the self. In the psychotic consciousness, as in the child's world and the nightmare world, anything can happen. Connections which might offer security are themselves felt as dangerous and are attacked: the meanings of words, the parts of the self, the relations between self and others. Other people may become enemy aliens, or at least suspect, because, in holding to sanity, they threaten the psychotic vision to which the self blindly clings for its apparent survival. But psychosis, of course, offers no safety, even when its vision is not in itself nightmarish, for the real world continues to exist and its meanings continue to threaten the psychotic self. In psychosis, each day's life is like trying to build a safe house in a hurricane, using crumbling sand and working with paralyzed hands; nothing holds together. Reality itself has become a nightmare.

Psychosis is not a mirror for our problems. As what our anxious age calls "normal neurotics," we can see there only this nightmare image of our own conflicts. Yet this vision can illuminate our own understanding of ourselves all the more easily because it is so graphic. To know psychosis can help us to know sanity. It can give us the security to look at ourselves clearly and in perspective, without being frightened by what we see—even when we find in ourselves feelings that would make us "crazy" *if* they were not contained within the structure of a basically rational self, a basically secure psychic house.

We all have fright and rage within ourselves. We all suffer, in certain ways, and at certain times and places, from anxiety, guilt, hostility, and depression. The safe house of the self can contain these feelings. In the safe house, our anxiety is restrained from filling every room with its poisonous gas, and our rage is restrained from knocking down the walls. Our feelings are mitigated by a sense of reality and a sense of proportion; they are securely located in the self and clearly related to situation an issue.

But awareness is the condition of this safety, and that is why we look at nightmare, at craziness, and at the scrambled perceptions of childhood, seeking their meaning to the daylight self, the rational self, the adult self. We can separate these realms of experience in order to describe them and to examine their nature. But we must come back to the fact that the person who dreams of monsters is the same person who gets up and goes to work in the morning. The anxious adult carries within herself the earlier self, the child who feared abandonment, chaos, and the murderous force of her own hostile wishes; the psychotic person was once, and may be soon again, a person to whom the world and the self were difficult but not impossible to encounter. When we try to split off and deny our own nightmares, fantasies, "childish" fears and "crazy" feelings, we only make them more powerful, for then we keep them shrouded in the protection of darkness, sheltered in the subterranean caves of the psyche. When we bring these monsters out into the light, we have the chance to neutralize and channel their power. When we enter the room in the self where the wild things are, we can begin to clear that space and make it safe.

But our task is not to totally banish our monsters, for they are also our friends, our fantasied representations of aspects of ourselves. As children master their fears by creating the friendly monster in stories and in their play, we as adults sense that the denomic aspect of the self is the basis of creative energy. Our task is not to deny or to inhibit the demonic but to accept it and to transmute its energy for human and social purposes. Fear of monsters is ultimately fear of being alive.

Unsafe Space: Anxiety and the Waking Dream

THREE

> *I have a monster inside me . . . What does the monster want? . . . It wants me to be loved, and only me.*
> *All the time, even when things are going well, I always keep feeling something is going to happen.*
> *I don't want to think about it.*
> *I feel like the future is a locked door, and I don't know what's waiting behind the door.*
> *I don't have any peace within myself.*

Nightmares don't end when we awaken; the guilt and dread of nightmare shadow our waking life. Fantasy is not confined to the hiding places of art and daydream, or to the distorted world of psychosis; it pervades each person's reality. Magic lies not only in the hopes and fears of children, but also deep in the emotions and expectations of the adult.

Just as the child comes screaming out of sleep, still seeing the monster in the room, we as adults bring nightmare feelings into our daylight world. The heavy sense of horror that sometimes follows a nightmare is only the overt form of this haunting. Our basic fears and guilts that are the original springs of nightmare also define our unsafe space in the daylight world.

Nightmares are often projected, by children and by cultures, as monsters that lie in wait for unwary wanderers—behind the tree, deep in the lake, up the mountainside, around the corner, in the basement, in the next neighborhood. The place where the monster lurks is identified as an unsafe place, a taboo zone, alien territory, off limits, no trespassing allowed. The child who disobeys, the person who is too free or too nonchalant, walks at his peril into this unsafe place. He may forget he is unsafe, and he may walk cheerfully—unguarded, distracted—but the creepy music in the film or the ominous sentence in the story reminds us of his foolishness and his danger.

In a comparable way, nightmare feelings and figures live not only at night inside a person's head, but also in places in the outside world where the person would normally feel free to go. For a very withdrawn person, the unsafe space may begin just outside the door of her room. She may not go out of the house or beyond the corner store, or she may not get into a car, because she feels that something terrible will happen if she does. A person less disturbed and less withdrawn will work and go shopping and do other ordinary things; but he will not drive the car into New York, or drive over a bridge, or go near a dog. To enter the unsafe places and situations reawakens nightmare feelings. The moves the person makes are circumscribed by an internal nightmare.

PHOBIAS

We are used to thinking of these nightmare-in-daylight feelings in their most specific form, as *phobias*. When we think of the monster lurking in a particular place or kind of place, we are close to the concept of phobia, the panic felt by some people in enclosed spaces, in open spaces, or in high places; or the intense fear of certain animals, who may take on a magical or symbolic meaning.

Phobias define unsafe space very precisely. Specific kinds of places or specific kinds of moves in the world are felt as profoundly unsafe. To visit these places or to make these moves means, as in folk tales; that one enters the realm of a monster. The "monster" is not thought of a such; but the anxiety lying in wait, ready to pounce on the person, is so powerful that it must be avoided at all costs: This anxiety guards the forbidden realm, signalling the person that he is out of bounds. To know that there is really no monster and nothing to be afraid of doesn't make the anxiety signals any less intense.

The person may be unable to go into an elevator, ride on a train, or climb an enclosed stairway. Therefore he cannot visit friends who live in apartments, shop in department stores, or look for work. The phobia must be accommodated, whatever it is the person wants to do. Sometimes such a person asks for therapy to rid himself of this problem. He will say, *I want to go to your office for help, but I can't leave the house,* or *I can't ride in a car.* The person is in mortal dread of subjecting himself to the phobic anxiety. When he falls prey to that anxiety, it feels as if he is dying.

ANXIETIES AND FEARS

We can extend the concept of phobia into a concept of unsafe space that is milder, less specific, less localized, more pervasive. A person may have an unease in going into strange rooms, an anxiety in quiet places, an inability to sit comfortably in a room with a group of people, a feeling of being unable to find his way to a strange place by following directions. We may be hearing this kind of anxiety when people say they "hate crowds" or "hate big parties" or "hate eating in restaurants" or "hate going into the city." These situations are defined as unsafe space, where relaxation and enjoyment become impossible. We can call this a matter of preference, of course; but distaste for an experience can also mask anxiety. The person may have a love for music or ballet, yet be unable to enter the forbidden zone of the theatre, the crowded street, the highway traffic, the unfamiliar environment of the city, because of the anxieties provoked by these unsafe space. There are, of course, real hazards in these places. But, for some people, the societal reality only confirms the inner sense of mortal danger.

We are not saying here that nightmares *cause* these daytime fears; but that the same fears and conflicts that provoke nightmare become a secret, unconscious organizer of the person's waking world. Experience is distorted by these fears; potential enjoyment is converted into forbidden fruit. These floating anxieties and selective fears of the waking life have the same sources as the monsters, bizarre figures, and events of the nightmare world. The person who is startled awake by a disturbing dream will have similar prickings of anxiety in the world of real experience—in buildings and vehicles, in the ocean when the waves come, in seeing a certain kind of animal, in certain kinds of social situations, in moments of potential intimacy and sharing, or perhaps when he is alone in his own house.

Fear and anxiety are often unconscious, although they may be conscious and may even dominate consciousness, crowding out everything else. *Fear* refers to something real, something tangible or definable which is identified as a threat. *Anxiety* is a state of unease that feels very much like fear; but it does not relate to a real, present danger, only to an imagined or fantasied one—or perhaps to a danger that could be real if it were not so remote in time, place, or likelihood.

In *fear*, a person reacts as an animal reacts to an enemy, and defends against the threat with an action or with flight. In *anxiety,* since the threat is much less present or much less clearly defined, so is the action that would mitigate it. The person cannot say exactly what arouses the anxious feeling, and therefore he cannot tell how to relieve it. The difference between fear and anxiety is like the difference between a thunderstorm and a thick fog. We know enough to seek shelter in a storm, and to emerge from shelter when it is ended. But in a fog, we are unsure of the path, we cannot find our way, and we imagine hidden dangers that cannot be identified; in a fog, we are afraid to move.

We like to use the world *fright* to describe a state of feeling that partakes of both fear and anxiety. Like the fog of anxiety in which motion is hesitant, fright is paralyzing. Fright can be thought of as a freezing of motion, like the freezing of deer caught by an auto's headlights. Fright is a traumatized condition, whether the trauma has been one incident or, as is more frequent, a long, repetitive series of incidents which have a cumulative meaning. The cumulative meaning is: *This impulse is unsafe; This experience is unsafe; This realm of experience is out of bounds.*

Fright has to do with experience which is desired, yet feared. A person may want a sexual relationship, yet he may feel anxious whenever he is alone with a woman. A person may want to make friends, but he may feel uncomfortable talking to others; or he may want to develop close friendships, but he always finds something going wrong. A person may want to achieve something in a field of interest, yet she always sabotages her own efforts. This happens because what the person consciously wants to do involves the expression of wishes he is afraid to acknowledge.

Anxiety is really an expression of ambivalence; it signals us when our wishes come into contact with our fright. Anxiety can signal real danger to the self, and it functions then as a guardian of our sanity and our integrity as a self. But anxiety can also give us false alarms, like leftover highway signs warning us of dangers that no longer exist. These signals, left standing on roads no longer unsafe for traffic, function as barricades to our growth.

Anxiety tells us of our wishes as well as of our fright. It tells us of the impulse that tempts the self into dangerous territory, the longing that threatens to overwhelm the self. This impulse or longing seduces us into the avoided realm of experience; but to carry out the impulse and have what we long for is felt as threatening. We do not dare to go forward into the experience; yet we cannot completely stay away. The person in this quandary is torn: The wish or impulse pushes him forward, the fright pulls him back.

THE MEANINGS OF ANXIETIES

What do these anxieties mean? We can distinguish three basic forms of anxiety, which can be described as paranoid anxiety, depressive anxiety, and guilt anxiety. Paranoid anxiety involves the underlying fear of attack, mutilation, or disintegration of the self. Depressive anxiety involves the fear of emptiness and loss. Guilt anxiety involves the fear of damage to important figures, either to other people in the real world of relationships, or to the earlier figures, usually of parents and siblings, who are carried within the self from childhood.

These underlying anxieties that plague us in confronting experience often show themselves in forms that seem, at first glance, remote from these basic meanings. But, once we understand these meanings and are sensitive to them, they can illuminate our behavior and our choices; and this in turn can help us to open up new realms of feeling and experience in ourselves and in the world.

For our specialized realms of fear and anxiety in daily life, like the nightmares that are their counterparts in sleep, are not singular, not merely insignificant quirks of an otherwise integrated personality. Rather, they are expressions of an underlying, more pervasive unease in the person, an extensive zone of fright. They hint of the person's unspoken terrors; they are clues to what goes on in silence, in the secret room of the self. They reflect the feelings of the self not only toward the *direct* reality of the street, the train, the ocean, the theater, the house, or the bed, but toward the *implied* possibilities of excitement, temptation, exposure, arousal, vulnerability, conflict, or damage—the dreaded overtones of sexuality and of violence which are hidden in our fears about the arousal of any feeling or excitement.

We use these words because the anxiety that constricts experience is, on one level, an anxiety about the release of feeling and impulse: It is an anxiety about loss of control. People who have grown up repressing their impulses and feelings imagine these impulses and feelings to be very dangerous. Like the wishes expressed in nightmare and in the child's magical thinking, they seem to carry the power to do unthinkable damage to ourselves and to others. The repressed feeling may be anger or grief or excitement. Whatever the feeling, its imagined power is greater than any probable effect in reality.

A woman says, *I'm afraid to cry, because I'm afraid I'll never stop.* A man says to his wife, *If I ever lost control and hit you, I'd probably kill you.* A couple, inwardly enraged and frustrated in their longing for each other's love, maintain silence or avoid each other by talking about commonplaces. People who have never dared to release their feelings don't get the chance to learn that their feelings are, in reality, limited in power. Adults who don't let themselves get excited—in sex, in love, in anger, in curiosity, in work—are like children for whom excitement is a mingling of joy and terror, both feelings so powerful that they seem overwhelming to the fragile ego. Because the feeling is never tested out in reality, the person never discovers that the feeling can be expressed or the impulse followed without disaster, without anyone's dying or going crazy.

Again, it is vital to recognize that our fears and our longings are merged in our unconscious experience. We wish on one level for what we fear on another, and we tremble at the power of our wishes. The man who is afraid to lose his temper really knows he harbors the unconscious, primitive wish to kill. What he doesn't know or trust is that the wish is under realistic control; it seems to him that to lose *any* control would be to lose *all* control, so he may be afraid even to argue with his wife, in case his repressed rage might break out in murderous assault. The person afraid to weep really wants to drown herself in grief, to dissolve herself and return to the comfort of the womb. Therefore she fears that to allow herself to "dissolve" even in the temporary relief of tears would mean the fulfillment of this wish and the permanent loss of her self and her self-control.

FANTASY AND EXPECTATION

These ambivalences create our unsafe space, the space of anxiety and conflict, within ourselves and in our relationships. Our fright is really a terror at what we call, in its most extended sense, the *primal scene*. The primal scene in this sense is the child's perception of what the parents do— to the child and to each other. This becomes the model of what people do to other people and to the self. It becomes the basis, not of our *realistic* expectations as adults, but of our *fantasies* about what will happen if we allow ourselves to go inside a feeling or an experience, or if we allow ourselves to get close to another person.

Our expectations are born of experience; but often the crucial experiences are buried in the childhood memory, and are permanently colored and distorted by childhood perceptions. Children can perceive and integrate only what their immature egos and their limited experience allow. The perceptions that are most frightening to children are, of course, the ones that are most distorted by their own fright and rage and by that of their parents. These frightening perceptions, these partially distorted pictures of what the parents are doing and what the child herself is doing, are powerful and persistent. These early images and shades of feeling become embedded in our unconscious expectations, our unconscious fantasy.

We have already spoken of what chilren imagine about the parents' sexuality, about their bodily intimacy, and about their "making" each other and making babies. The child, not only when he asks questions about sex, but in all his daily experience with his parents, is forming both impressions and fantasies of what really happens between a man and a woman, and between these adult figures and himself.

Suppose the parents are always quarreling bitterly, with loud, angry voices and poisonous words. The child takes in the rage and, on the level of fantasy, feels that the parents are killing each other. Depending on his age, on the intensity of the quarrel, and on how far the parents go in acting out their rage, he may fear, each time they quarrel, that they really *will* kill each other. Suppose, on the other hand, that the parents never argue but live together in silent hostility. This, too, the child picks up as a rage; and perhaps this is all the more threatening because, like any repressed feeling, it is never expressed in a realistic, limited frame of reference, but lurks in the shadows of fantasy where wishes are omnipotent. Like the man afraid to argue with his wife because of his own repressed violence, the child may sense violence in his parents and constantly fear its fatal outbreak.

Suppose one parent dominates the other and always "cuts off" the other's wants, preferences, and opinions. The child will carry this image of what a man does to a woman or a woman to a man; and this will be his adult expectation, in fantasy, of what will happen in a man-woman relationship; He will cut off his mate, or allow himself to be cut off, or, if the fantasy is frightening enough, he will avoid man-woman relationships altogether. If the child himself is "cut off" and punished or ignored whenever he asserts himself or expresses a feeling, this will be his fantasy expectation in adult life, unless or until it is partly corrected in his other relationships.

This is how it comes about that relationships, for some people, are a taboo zone, a realm of experience roped off by fantasy. Bad experience in the family carries not one but two bad messages. One message is: *This bad, painful, damaging behavior is what people do to each other.* And the other, more subtle message is: *It's not safe to do anything else, either.* The first message is clear in the behavior of the parents. The second message is delivered by implication. If father and mother only fight, or only avoid each other, or only work, or only run from one thing to another, or only stay close to home and have no friends, they imply to the child that to live differently would be either dangerous or not worth doing.

Parents exert very powerful controls on children by implying that certain kinds of behavior are out of bounds. That is how children are socialized: They are taught what is and is not acceptable to the family, what is and is not gratifying, what is and is not a promising path to follow, what is and is not "normal" behavior, what is and is not what people do together. Parents in their teaching and children in their learning depend heavily on these social and family patterns.

But not all the parent's socializing of the child is on a conscious level. Many messages are transmitted to children without or in spite of the parents' intention. If the parents are fearful or feel inadequate in certain realms of experience, the fear is transmitted to the child. To the extent that the child has bad emotional experiences in the family, he learns to fear new experience at the same time as he learns fright at whatever is traumatizing in the everyday familial experience. The damage and loss that is felt and feared in the family becomes the damage and loss that is expected in all other relationships. This expectation is not realistic, but it can be self-confirming. The negative expectation is often unconscious. To the extent that it lies at the level of unconscious fantasy, it is less accessible to the rational self, and therefore more powerful.

We must never underestimate the power of parental fantasy, and of childhood fantasy carried into adulthood. Much of the work of psychotherapy lies in clearing unconscious fantasy out of the person's expectations, memories, and perceptions of the present. Fantasy in the sense we are involved with here is not mere daydreaming, set apart from "real life," but a way of seeing that colors and distorts experience to a more or less serious degree. The fantasy expectation of damage in relationships, or of damage if the self loses control in feeling, is very powerful and constricting. If it is not countered by clarifying reflection and by corrective experience, it can cripple a person throughout life.

The fantasies we are speaking of are really, in their depths, fantasies about our own bodies and those of others; and to remember this can help us to remember their power. When we speak of "cutting off" a person's statements or self-assertions, we are not far from what we know, in theories of child development now widely accepted, as the fear of castration. Or, when a mother cannot allow a child to separate from her at an appropriate age, and when the child in turn cannot separate himself, the feeling of emptiness, loss, and panic when separation does occur is also of the body—a feeling that the child is an appendage to the mother's body or that he cannot survive outside the womb of her influence.

We can see this connection clearly when we look at the two-year-old child, clinging to its mother, and then at the schizophrenic young adult physically clinging to the workers who care for her. This is the same anxiety that may cause a less disturbed person to remain in the parent's home well into adulthood. Or perhaps she will not marry; or she may make her own home a block away from mother, or call her mother every day, or never venture far from her mother's opinions. These are all shades of anxiety evoked by the fear of separation. There are crucial differences of degree, but the root of the problem remains the same. The fantasy in its most extreme form is: *If I am not attached to mother's body, I will die and she will die;* the corresponding fantasy of the mother is also: *Separation means death.* Adults whose parents cannot allow separation sometimes develop severe guilt feelings around the illness of a parent. Some parents whose "children" have grown into adults attempt to keep them in the position of children; and they may have somatic reactions such as heart attacks whenever the grown "child" asserts independence. The message *If you leave me you will kill me* is thereby reinforced in a very concrete form, and the admixture of reality in the fantasy elicits a devastating guilt.

Again, everyone lives in such unconscious fantasy to some degree. Fantasy in this sense is not apart from life, not merely a daydream punctuating reality. It is also a veil that clouds our perceptions, or a lens that distorts them. In fantasy, we look at another person and see in that person a remembered parent or sibling or an imagined lover. In fantasy, strangers may be seen as enemies, and all our experience may be viewed "through a glass darkly." In fantasy, any other woman may be seen as a rival, any other man as a threat. These fantasies filter our "real" experience; and one of the perpetual and difficult tasks of psychotherapy, as of our own introspection, is to distinguish the shapes of reality. Sometimes the crucial difference is in perspective and proportion, as if we are looking through rippled glass that magnifies some elements of experience and diminishes others.

It sounds extreme to say that one person approaching another in daily life has fantasies of killing or being killed, devouring or being devoured, being pushed out or being trapped and smothered. But the presence of these unconscious fantasies is often confirmed when people begin to explore their real feelings. If we say to someone, for example: *If you say "No", will your mother die of it?* or *You got angry and nobody died,* the response is often a slightly embarrassed laugh of recognition: *I guess that's what I was afraid of.*

We can understand this better if we remember that the relatively mature, rational adult self is constructed over time by the structuring, limiting, channeling, and integration of the vital energies of the organism as it grows. The adult self is not a replacement for the earlier, primitive self, as the "baby" teeth are replaced by the "grown-up" teeth. Rather, the child body/self develops into the adult body/self in a long, complex, often uneven, but basically continuous process. We change but we remain the same. We are all children who have grown into adults; we are all primitive thinkers who have become more or less rational; we are all organisms who have developed more or less fully the elaborate equipment of the human being. We are more vulnerable, more primitive, and more dominated by fantasy at one end of this long continuum than at the other. But we never stop needing to be fed, never stop having primitive wishes, never totally stop being afraid. We never entirely stop seeing through eyes that are clouded by our fantasies, our wishes, and our fears.

This means that, on one level, we remain transfixed by the primal scene of the interactions of our parents, seen through our childhood eyes. The symptoms of this fright are not isolated, and we can work to understand them in their context of symbolic meaning. If a person dreams about drowning, the meaning of it is not just a literal fear of water that may keep the person from learning how to swim. The meanings of the dream may extend into fears of motion, of loss of control, of sexual rhythms, of being flooded with mother's feelings, of going deeply into anything lest the self be dissolved. If a person dreams about a town where everything is destroyed and everyone is gone, this may relate to the feeling he has, in his waking life, of pushing everyone away and destroying everything he touches with his hostility. If he too is to be killed in the dream, this may express the reciprocal punishment he feels he deserves and will receive from others.

We are speaking here in simple terms of meanings that are extremely complex for each person. This is not to say that dreams and feelings should be analyzed casually or simplistically. But it should give us hope to realize that our underlying feelings are expressed in ways that we can learn to understand. Our moods and our dreams are not visitations from some alien source, nor are they meaningless aberrations. They are our own coded messages to ourselves about the experiences we both desire and fear. To understand these messages can help us to make our choices conscious and viable, to express our wishes within the framework of reality, and to diminish our unnecessary fears. Otherwise, we remain prisoners of our inexpressible wishes and our unmanageable fright.

Fright holds us frozen beneath the level of consciousness, because fright is something no one wants to feel. Therefore we know fright primarily in its effects, whether on others or within ourselves. We know fright when we "clam up" or have trouble breathing, contract the stomach muscles or the sphincter, develop back or neck pain, close the throat, or hysterically lose hearing, sight, or the ability to move. These are all possible bodily reactions to fright that may be conscious or unconscious, chronic or acute.

Inhibition, over-caution, and closed-mindedness are other, more subtle kinds of tightening. They mean that the body and the psyche cannot move freely, cannot express feeling or explore experience freely—with a basic feeling of being safe.

Fright shows itself most clearly in this bodily and psychic freezing. But there are other signs by which we can know its presence. When we see a person avoid certain kinds of experience, then we know fright is present. The person has learned: *This area is roped off; this space is unsafe.* The person may feel that the experience will lead into feelings of inadequacy, or into sexual or aggressive feelings which threaten to go out of control and overwhelm the "rational" self. Or the person may feel that the experience will provoke disapproval, or it may threaten the person with loss of his own self-image, or with loss of a relationship that is emotionally important and desired even though it is constricting.

Therefore this conflict-ridden situation is avoided. The person says: *I feel shut out of this part of life;* but at the same time he conveys the message: *I don't want this experience; I don't dare to get involved in it; I'm afraid.* This same message may be masked as: *That's boring; That's a waste of time; I don't need that; It's too expensive; I'm not that kind of person; I haven't time for that; Remember, I have to work; I can't make that scene.* Instead of testing out the experience that is half-desired and half-feared, the person escapes it by avoidance.

Avoidance itself can take many forms. Some of them involve the insidious forms of psychic mechanisms and defenses which are, in the long run, damaging to the self, and yet which have been, for the growing and embattled self, a way to survive. We will go more deeply into these habitual means of survival in the next chapter, for they are prominent in the behavior of anxious, conflicted people, and they are seriously depriving in their effects. Perhaps the most important thing we can know of the repetitive mechanisms of avoidance and defense is that they prevent *corrective* experience. Repetition interferes with learning new ways to fill emptiness, to resolve conflict, and to replace bad experience with good. Often this corrective experience cannot take place without the help of psychotherapy; and even that help has limits to its effectiveness.

But we know that hope lies in awareness of ourselves and our own motives and conflicts; and that our ability to respond to others lies in our understanding of their needs. Whatever is needed to achieve that awareness, and to achieve the changes in behavior that can accompany understanding, is a part of what we need as human beings in our long struggle to become ourselves and to live in the light of reality. Otherwise, we are trapped in fantasy and its endlessly mirrored repetitions, and to that extent we inhabit a waking dream.

Unsafe Space: The Flight from the Self

FOUR

> *All day long, I'm running. That's the way life is today.*
> *It's good for right now, but it won't last—I know it.*
> *I think I'm going to split, man.*

Anxiety reinforces itself. Left unattended, anxiety partitions the house of the self into corridors leading to barricaded rooms—endless corridors down which we run in repetitive cycles of fright and flight, glimpsing in mirrors the alarming reflection of our own fears. Anxiety closes the way to safe space; it is a path of avoidance and disconnection within the self. It makes us tremble and fumble as we try to form the links that would lead us out of danger. It means retreat from the path of comprehension and clarity.

There is no escape from the fact that all involvement in life, and all knowledge of ourselves, entails some anxiety and conflict. Only in fantasy can we wish to eliminate stress. Our hopes are directed rather to the restructuring and recreation of the self in such a way that stress is handled with more satisfaction and less destruction of experience.

For there is enormous, continual, daily destruction going on in the life of a person who is running away from the self. Experience is destroyed, feeling is destroyed, opportunity for change is destroyed before it can arise, and perception itself is destroyed before it can touch the self with its burden of pain.

THE PATTERNS OF THE MANIC DEFENSE

We are concerned here with patterns of avoidance, and specifically with the many forms of what we call the *manic defense*. Here we are using the term "manic" in its most extended sense and not in its more specific meaning as "manic-depressive illness." The manic pattern as a defense has its relationships to the psychotic manic state, and also to "normal" euphoric states of feeling. But it is also definably different, in ways which we will explore.

When we speak, in daily life, of a person being "manicky" we usually mean that he is having a flight of high spirits; the person has "left the ground" in a sense, and enjoys a euphoria in which he ignores, for the moment, any unpleasant aspects of reality. There is an excitement, an agitation, in which the person has a sense of moving at a more rapid pace, going beyond himself in a flight of humor or a surge of activity. The person may feel brighter, wittier, more able, more sparkling. Words and ideas come faster. The person's sense of what he can do and be is lifted and extended beyond its usual context, and freed of its usual limits and hindrances.

We all have "highs" as well as "lows" in the normal fluctuation of our feelings. We all have times when we feel that *Everything is good,* and other times when everything seems to be going wrong. When we are feeling that *Everything is good* we are not really denying reality, but we are holding aside, for the moment, any thoughts and concerns that would disturb our sense of euphoria, that would bring us "down to earth" to dwell on our troubles and our cares.

But there are differences among our "highs." We may have times of intense joy—what Maslow called "peak experiences"—perhaps in falling in love, or in giving birth to a child, or in coming into physical contact with the natural world. These experiences take over our emotions in a very natural way; they are not defenses, but are grounded in the realities of our lives. Yet they blot out, for the time being, the remainder of our reality. They are like a bright sun, wholly taking our attention from the shadows.

There are plateaus of happiness, too, in which we feel that *Everything is good* because of real satisfactions in our lives. There are times in life when we have everything we need, and we know we have it—good love, good work, good friends, a true sense of happiness and of emotional safety that is not evanescent, but is founded upon real experience, built up over time. We can have euphoric moods that are founded upon this true happiness, in which we are not really denying the presence of any problems, but in which we are suffused with the sense that *Life is good*—so that, again, the cares and problems of every day are put aside.

But there are many people who live on "highs" that do not rest on a sense of reality but which are a denial of the person's real experience, an attempt to mask it. We can see this most clearly in a person who depends on the artificial highs produced by liquor or drugs. These artificial stimulants can be used to enhance good experience that is real, as at a party or in the company of friends. On the other hand, they can be used to create the illusion of good feelings in a person who is otherwise sunk in bad feelings: the illusion of fellowship in a person who lives in fright, the illusion of being fed in a person who feels empty, the illusion of life in a person who feels dead.

When liquor or drugs are used to blot out reality, then sooner or later the bad feelings of the self take over again, and with a vengeance. The person who tries to wash away her troubles with alcohol may end the night raging or weeping like a child, and spend the next day drowned in her own depression. The person who lives on "speed" rides a roller coaster back into depression that is deepened by the draining of the body's real resources. Speed kills. The person who seeks the comfort of addictive drugs lays himself open to experiences that are ever more remote from the reality of the whole self; the "highs" or the periods of calm are transient and ever more difficult to achieve. At the extremes of addiction, the body is ravaged and the self destroyed.

When we consider the highs that are not created by chemicals, but which are the product of our emotional processes, we can make the same crucial distinction between those states of feeling that enhance real experience and those that deny reality. The essential questions are: *What is the basis of the good feeling?* and *What place does it have in this person's life?*

This doesn't mean that everything in reality must be good in order for a person to have good feelings that are realistically based. Suppose a person is unemployed. He may have spells of optimism and even enthusiasm, based on actively tackling the problem and finding that new possibilities are opening up. This is different from rushing around in a state of excitement, spending one's energies talking about the problem, pacing the floor with obsessive thoughts, or taking actions that are not the real steps involved in finding a job. It is also different from sitting at home, saying to oneself and to others: *Today I have no prospects, but tomorrow a wonderful job is going to find me.*

Suppose a person is having trouble forming and maintaining a love relationship. He can still enjoy euphoric good feeling based on having good sex in the context of a brief or partial relationship. But this is different from giving birth to an instant fantasy that this relationship will now fill the whole of life, satisfy all needs, and last forever.

This escape into fullblown fantasy from a reality of impoverished experience is what we call a manic state in a "normal-neurotic" sense. This state of mind is not psychotic; yet it is certainly not well grounded in reality. It involves a faulty map and clock of interpersonal and social space and time. This state of mind denies that experience involves steps to be taken and stages to be lived through. It is a fantasy of instant gratification, a flight from a reality that seems too difficult to handle: the reality that includes failure as well as success, and bad feelings as well as good.

Many people try to live their lives by creating a series of such manic states, which of course involve a continual, draining effort to shore up their defenses and wall out reality. Even then, they must suffer, between the episodes of manic fantasy, the spaces of despair, in which they come into contact with the exaggerated reality of their own failures and problems. Time is either too fast or too heavy.

The psychic house of a person involved in this process is like a "railroad" apartment—a series of confined rooms without windows, none of them to be lingered in for long. The room of manic fantasy is decorated for quick stimulation, but it is not furnished for a long stay; it has only artificial light, and offers no nourishing food. It exits only into a hollow space of disillusion, again a confined place, crowded with the ghosts of past failures, empty of comfort, with no ray of light or realistic hope. The person flees from this room; but again the only exit is into the cell of another manic state—with *its* only exit, in turn, into another space of despair.

In another related form of what we call the manic defense, the malady is more subtle, more congruent with societal values, and equally chronic. This is the pattern of perpetual activity which is not permitted to involve the deeper feelings of the self. It is another kind of running away—a flight from experience that takes the form of moving too fast to be held—of skimming over the surface of experience in order not to sink into its depths.

The person employing this kind of manic defense does not appear frozen or in fright. On the contrary, he is always in motion—but the motion is that of one foot moving out the door of the experience. The person is afraid to be involved; involvement is felt as damaging. The person is afraid to be touched; the touch is felt as an assault. The person is afraid to be held; to be held is to be caught, trapped, overpowered. The nightmare that dominates fantasy is of being chased, caught, and killed. The defense is a perpetual running away. Such a person remains divided, feeling: *I don't want to commit myself* or *This is not mine.*

In the state of mind structured by manic defenses, the person is afraid to make contact with another or with the reality of the self. To know the self, let alone to show its reality to another, is to unveil what is felt to be a Medusa which will freeze others and the self into a permanent terror.

Instead, the person knows no choice but to run away within the self—to hide, to avoid, to split off, and to deny the nightmare figures and the nightmare feelings. These nightmare figures represent the wishes, fears, longings, and rages we dare not perceive, because they are felt to be more powerful than the self, and threatening to survival. The nightmare feelings—of being trapped, being chased, being found out, being bitten, being swallowed, being abandoned, being helpless, doing and suffering damage and killing—are expressed, in the daytime life, in the use of the manic defense, a flight into another kind of fantasy.

In the manic defense, part of the fantasy is that the person has no trouble, no bad feelings, no problems, no bad memories. This seemingly "good" fantasy is laid over the nightmare fantasy that says *Everything I do is bad; I am bad; I destroy everything I touch.* Such a person feels *I am perfect,* and *Everyone envies me* in order that he may avoid feeling, *I am nothing, and I envy everyone.*

THE FLIGHT FROM UNMANAGEABLE FEELINGS

The person who resorts to the manic defense has enormous guilt and enormous fear of the self. The manic state is an attempt to run away from the bad in the self. For the most part this guilt and fear have to do with "bad" feelings and "bad" thoughts toward other people.

Most of us are not murderers, rapists, or robbers. But all of us have desires, however fleeting or unconscious, to kill, to steal, to do or to take what we want without limit or restraint. To feel guilty about these impulses is part of the child's development of conscience. The omnipotent wish gives way to the child's fear of "being bad," and to the shame and guilt these wishes inspire.

As adults, much of our guilt and fear is the result of a kind of psychic overkill. Many of us, instead of being taught merely to limit our wishes and feelings on the level of behavior, are taught to repress them. Angry feelings are treated as if they were attacks in action. Angry actions in turn are treated as physical assaults, and physical acting out as if it were murderous. For many people, rage is so frightening that no negative feeling can be allowed—in the self, in the mate, or in the child.

Negative feelings generally are a problem for most of us. Very often children are unable to express anger, sadness, or feelings of criticism toward their parents. These feelings are often chopped off by parents, because they make the parents anxious. The parents don't want to receive these bad feelings; they themselves don't want to be accused of being bad. Instead they criticize the child, overtalk the child, cut off the child, make the child into the bad one. This makes the child feel there is something wrong with expressing angry or aggressive feelings. It seems that bad feelings are to be hidden and denied. Psychotherapy is often necessary to correct this process of automatic hiding and denying.

Everybody has good feelings and bad feelings. We need them. We need negative feelings in order to make space for ourselves, to set limits, and to push people away when they are damaging us. Our sexuality, too, is based upon a fusion of sensuality and empathy with our aggression. Without aggression, we can't put the whole self into anything, nor can we hold anything for the self. When our bad feelings must be withheld, hidden, and denied, then our good feelings too are withheld; the whole self is muted, attenuated, partialized.

When parents perpetually give the response: *You're angry at me?—You're bad; You're saying No to me?—You're bad; You hate your brother and sister?—You're bad,* then the child learns to deny and mistrust himself. Children, of course, don't express themselves in moderation. Children don't say to their mothers, *I don't like what you just did;* they say, *You're the worst mommy in the whole world and I hate you,* or *Mommy always blames me and you get everything and I'll never play with you again.* The child is saying to his parent or sibling, *You're a monster.* The message he needs to hear back is *You're angry and I'm angry, but you're not a monster and I'm not a monster.* When the parent says, in words, action, or tone of voice, *You're bad to have such feelings and you're killing me with your angry words and you're killing your brother by hitting out and what you're saying is wrong and crazy and don't let me hear anymore,* the parent is saying *You're a monster* right back, and joining the child in the exaggerated world of fantasy.

Children also learn to be afraid of their bad feelings if they are given too much scope in behavior. The child who feels no one will limit the outbreak of his rage is reinforced in the feeling of dangerous, excessive power. As he is in danger of really doing harm, he has all the more reason to fear the rampaging monster in himself.

People also may grow up feeling that sadness is unacceptable, futile, something to be hidden and denied. Parents who have a need to "make nice" and to deny their own feelings are uncomfortable with a child's sadness and crying. They may rush to distract the child, to get her to quiet her sorrow and show a happier face. Or they may convey the message, *I don't care that you're hurt; I don't care they you're unhappy,* causing the child to feel that to try to get comfort is pointless, and that to try not to feel the pain, or to convert it into rage, is the best way to handle the feeling.

Again, we are speaking in simple terms of complex dynamics of growth. There is no easy formula for producing a healthy, integrated adult; and parents in any case act from their own constellation of positive and negative feelings, mature intentions, fantasy, and unmet needs. But we hope to develop helpful guidelines. It is clear in our experience that denied feelings fester in the deeper levels of the self. Sometimes these feelings reach explosive levels or become the source of unconscious conflict and unexplained depression. Sometimes people succeed, for long periods of time, in avoiding the kinds and levels of experience that would reawaken these feelings, which were unmanageable to the child and her parents and therefore seem inexpressible in adult life. There are the kinds of feelings that make people afraid to be in touch with themselves or to get involved and stay involved in relationships. People who feel that their bitterness, their sadness, their fright, and their unexpressed anger are unacceptable feel a necessity to hide, to avoid, to run away from themselves and from others, and to maintain the manic defense.

The manic state and its activity are compulsive; that is how we can distinguish them from a good state of mind and from good activity. A person says: *I'm always on the go. I'm always running. I don't have time to see my friends. I don't have time to spend with my wife. There are always too many things to do. I never have time for myself.* Or we may hear of someone: *She just can't do enough for a friend; He spends all his time helping others; Her children are her whole life; He's into everything.*

Such a person may say, *Well, is there something wrong with being active? That's the way I am;* or, *Is there something wrong with being a devoted parent/friend/citizen?* Of course there is nothing wrong with activity or with commitment; again, the compulsive quality is what makes the difference. That is what identifies the activity as flight from the deeper levels of the self.

The person using the manic defense may show this compulsive quality by the excess or by the lack of proportion in what he does. He is out at meetings, not one or two nights a week, but every night; she is earning, not one master's degree, but another and then another. The house is not just kept neat or even beautified, but is allowed to consume all of one's time, money, and energy. The person is always out shopping, feverishly hunting bargains, or simply roving restlessly through the stores. Work is expanded and tasks are multiplied, or social life is kept going constantly and in repetitive forms which allow no intimacy with others. Money is earned through a constant, killing pace of work effort—often fueled by the exchange of manicky enthusiasm that is rampant in such occupational fields as sales, advertising, and "show biz"; but it is spent as quickly, in ways as frantic, repetitive, and devoid of real satisfaction as the work itself. The person may feel he is on a treadmill or a merry-go-round, but that he doesn't know how to get off.

The aim of all this seemingly meaningless activity is to make sure that the person will never have to sit still and receive his or her own feelings. Often there is an underlying depression that the activity belies but cannot banish, so that to sit still brings home the feeling of loss and futility. For, in the frantic effort to get out of the self and "into everything," the self is scattered and lost. That is at once the aim and the tragic outcome of the manic defense in the forms we have described.

Again, we are not talking here of the psychosis that is psychiatrically diagnosed as "manic-depressive" but are using the word *manic* in a much looser and more extended sense. Still, as with other symptomatic behavior, we can see the milder and the more severe forms of the problem of a continuum, rather than as different in kind. The person in the psychotic form of the manic state may go on a spending spree that totally ignores financial reality; or he may talk incessantly, with a fountain of ideas constantly bursting inside his head; or he may physically show the overwhelming quality of his excitement by pacing the room, unable to sit still. In the "manic-depressive illness" this manic state alternates with severe depression, in which there is no ray of light—just as, in the manic state, there is no ray of darkness allowed to come into unconsciousness.

By contrast, for the person fully in touch with reality, experience is always mixed, and the person sees himself realistically as a mixture of "good" and "bad" characteristics. The integrated self takes in and contains both good and bad feelings. But, when a person has not been allowed to express her bad or negative feelings, she also cannot receive and contain them. The person learns to treat certain feelings as bad and cannot allow himself to express them or, therefore, to feel them. The feelings become threatening, and have to be viewed as alien, as not part of the self. This is the foundation of the splitting off of bad feelings and their projection onto other people.

THE MANIC FANTASY

The essence of the manic defense is *flight* from these bad feelings of the self. The manic state is based on the fantasy: *If I keep moving, I can escape the bad. The bad does not reside in myself, but in others.* From this perspective on the manic pattern of hectic activity, we can now take another look at the states of manic fantasy with which we began our discussion of manic defenses. The essential meaning of these patterns is the same: flight.

Running away can be done in slow motion. Sometimes we see a person who goes from one romance to another, and then to another. Each new person is idealized and seen as the solution to all problems. Each relationship is seen as *This time it's different,* meaning, *This time there will be no bad,* no negative feeling to cope with. Of course this fantasy can never be translated into reality. People, relationships, and life situations are never perfect, just as the self remains always a mixture of "good" and "bad." For the person in this defensive, manic flight from real experience, each new relationship means a bitter disappointment, because the basic fantasy that is its premise—*This time everything is good*—can never be fulfilled.

The manic flight means that real experience is continually destroyed—and that the bad in the self is continually denied. In looking at others and at the world first, the bad is denied, so that the hope of fantasy can settle on a person or situation; and then the good is denied, so that the new ground can be abandoned and the flight begin again. The hope of paradise or of the womb that is repeatedly aroused gives way again and again to a disillusionment that destroys all relationship and connection. Real experience cannot be allowed to take place because the person can live only with ideal images. To live with reality means to receive bad feelings, and to feel then in the self, and to integrate them into the whole of the self and the whole of a relationship.

This is exactly what the person cannot do who has not been allowed to express bad feelings and to learn how to handle them with others and within the self. The bad feelings are felt as monsters; other people are seen as monsters; and a relationship or situation that calls them forth becomes a phobic zone, a realm of wild things. No one can remain where he feels at the mercy of monsters; the only recourse is flight.

A tragic corollary to the manic escape is that nothing can be built up over time. Money can't be saved; it can only be spent. Time can't be structured to do good things for the self; it can only be killed, dismembered, or frozen in the bank. The person's skills and capacities cannot be gradually developed; he cannot "make something of himself." Instead, he must leap into opportunities which are insubstantial, building houses on sand that sifts away under his feet. Relationships cannot be constructed over time, incorporating the good and the bad in the self and the other person, making a truly safe space for the reality of each person: The person runs away in panic before this can take place.

This means that the involvement of the self in experience is very thin and very shallow. Real involvement always means risk. The person whose life has presented much bad and frightening experience, and who has learned only to run away, perceives involvement as a danger to the self.

It follows that those life situations that call for involvement are felt as especially dangerous. A love relationship, or a relationship with one's child, or an effort to achieve something, or a commitment to work one cares about, or real membership in a group, or participation in a movement for social change, or involvement in psychotherapy or in therapeutic work on one's marriage—any of these threaten some defenses of the self. To a person accustomed to using the manic defense, it feels safer to run away. The person refuses to penetrate experience and to let experience penetrate the self. He goes through life in a plastic wrapping, feeling the world as an airless, plastic bubble, an artificial womb.

But reality always tempts us toward involvement. The reality of our own needs demands real experience, not the chronic malnutrition of plastic food. We need to receive both good and bad feelings in order to be in contact with ourselves and with other people. We need to suffer the bad in order to enjoy the good. To avoid experience takes as much effort and as much struggle as would the effort to submerge oneself in it, to suffer and survive reality and make it into something gratifying. Conrad's Stein, in *Lord Jim,* says,

> A man that is born falls into a dream like a man who falls into the sea. If he tries to climb out into the air as inexperienced people endeavor to do, he drowns. . . . The way is to the destructive element submit yourself, and with the exertions of your hands and feet in the water make the deep, deep sea keep you up. So if you ask me—how to be? . . . there is only one way . . . In the destructive element immerse.

This immersion in experience takes courage and it takes effort; but the opportunity is always there, and the possibility of a fortunate seduction into involvement is ever present. For we are always drawn back into the effort to try to fulfill our needs, and this fulfillment lies in reality, and in corrective experience. This may involve the corrective experience of psychotherapy. It does involve the corrective experience of relationships and efforts in which we attempt not to repeat old experience, not to remain in the waking dream of repetitive fantasy and apprehension, but to gradually alter the element in which we live.

But the power of repetition is great, and realizing this can help us to understand the persistence of manic defense patterns. For the person who has suffered bad experience as a child, the only ways he knows of being closely involved with another person are painful, damaging ways. Even being in contact with the self puts the person in touch with painful feelings of being damaged and of doing damage. It seems easier and safer to skim over the surface of experience, and not to risk immersion.

The person who says, as so many people say today, *I don't want to get involved* is really saying *I don't trust my own inner world* and also, as we can see clearly when this is said in a city street, *I don't trust the world of others*. The inner world of feeling is felt to be dangerous, and so is the outer world of others and their actions. When a person says *I don't want to get involved,* this is likely to mean: 1) The person is not in good contact with the self and the feelings of the self; 2) the person is not fully involved in relationships, even with a mate or a child; 3) the person is not fully involved in the work he does; and 4) the person is not fully involved in the community or the society.

Some of the mistrust of one's inner world has its source in the concept of the Family Romance. The Family Romance is a complex corkscrew process. It begins in the child's feeling of betrayal by the parent, and with rejection of parental sexual intercourse, with its correlative facts of birth and death. The child refuses to be the excluded product of parental sex and to be an animal fated to live and die in a body. The child refuses to be a mere sibling and instead produces an idealized fantasy. In this fantasy, the child becomes an orphan, misplaced by accident in a family not his own, merely awaiting re-adoption by the King and Queen. Unfortunately, such idealization produces a terrible sense of guilt about betraying, rejecting, and killing off the real family, and a split in the self between idea and present reality. In this way, the betrayed child becomes the betraying adolescent, traitor to his family, avenger of the primal scene.

This dual process of being betrayed or expelled from the garden of Eden of infancy and then being the idealizing betrayer creates a structure of mistrust of self and others. Clinically, it emerges in the form of the mate who *knows* he or she cannot trust the marital partner, because the unconscious memory of being betrayed sexually by the parent, and of then betraying the parent through the fantasy of the ideal parent, means that no one is in good faith. Self-betrayal is the final act of the Family Romance. Sometimes a mate commits adultery as a preventive against anticipated betrayal. Sometimes a mate suffers adulterous betrayal to confirm the victim role and to avoid the guilt of the fantasy of betraying the other.

The Family Romance is thus the main interference with genuine marriage as well as the main psychological cause of divorce. The Family Romance causes a division in self-identity, with both the child's sense of victimage and the adolescent's retaliatory idealization blocking adult integration and the realization of trust and love. Rejection of the other becomes the only safe space.

History, as we will see in the final chapter, can be seen as a Family

Romance of Corporate Groups. In their internal and external relations, nation states are dominantly guided by Family Romance constructs. The FBI and the CIA are both defensive and offensive expressions of betrayal fantasies and realities. They simultaneously avenge betrayal, guard idealizations, and commit acts of betrayal. Such institutionalization of pre-adult psychic processes makes unreality more real than human reality. The world becomes divided into victims, betrayers and idealists who betray flesh and blood in the service of ideals. All bring childhood fantasy and childhood defenses into play.

The patterns of the manic defense tend to become chronic; the person tends to withhold the self, not in just one area, but in all areas. There are people, of course, who totally occupy themselves with work, and this becomes part of their defense against emotional and family experience. But this kind of involvement can only be with parts of the self, for only parts of the self, or certain levels of the self, are being fed. When the self is withheld from a full involvement in life, some of the feelings of the self are mired in childhood or in the persistence of fantasy. The person is "stuck," because the whole self cannot move into the world of the mature adult. The part of the self that remains in childhood or in fantasy or in nightmare tends to be hidden and denied, and any experience that might bring it into the light of day is instinctively avoided.

The person who flees from one romance into another is afraid of a real love relationship and its attendant feelings of anxiety; the possibility of rejection, loss, betrayal, damage to the self or to the other—and most of all the recognition of bad feelings in the self—seem to be too much to handle. The person who avoids full involvement in work or in the society takes the attitude, *Nothing I do will be recognized* or *Nothing I do can change the system,* partly because the threat of failure, the sense of helplessness, the fear of challenging authority, and the feeling *I am nobody* have been impressed upon the self by the early experience in the family.

A person who avoids involvement, when he comes to talk about problems with a mate, may say not only, *I have these problems with my wife and I think I should have chosen a different person,* but also *I'm not sure I'll stay in the marriage, and I'm not even sure that marriage is for me.* A person who withholds involvement with her child may be saying, on a deeper level, *I wish I had different children* or *I wish I wasn't a parent; I'm not really through with being a child, myself.* The person who feels persecuted in a job may explain his not making any effort to change things by saying *I don't know if I'll be there very long.* A person may deny the reality of a destructive marriage by "playing games" and then coming to a therapy session laughing about the games that are played. A person may present herself for therapy, yet she may not really bring her whole self to the effort, feeling secretly, *I'm here, but this is a lot of garbage, and I won't take it home with me.*

In this way a person can be ostensibly involved in a life situation, yet not really inside the experience. The person is always "of it but not in it." The full feeling of the relationship cannot be received, contained, and held, because some of it seeps out through the escape hatch in the back of the person's mind: *Maybe I'll find somebody else; Maybe I'll get a divorce; Maybe what we're doing is useless anyway; This isn't really real; It doesn't matter; This isn't going to be the whole of my life; My heart isn't in it; My mind is elsewhere; Maybe I'll split; Maybe I'm not really here.*

This is very different from feeling in the self: *I am really involved in this, and bringing my self to it. Maybe it will succeed and maybe it will fail; but in the meantime this is my life, and this is me living it, and I will receive and take in what it brings to me.* Yet many people keep themselves tied to lovers or friends or work or a marriage that can only satisfy part of the self, because of the fear of taking in real feeling. There is no full effort and no full relaxation. Unlike the children's dancing song that says finally *I put my whole self in,* or even *I take my whole self out,* they go through life saying *I put in only a part of myself and I'm not sure about that part either.* In this way they avoid the dangers of rejection, loss, and emptiness, as well as the suffering of damage and the guilty suffering of doing damage to others.

But there is no fatigue like the fatigue of flight; that is indeed "the loneliness of the long-distance runner." There is no unease like the tension of being poised for flight. There is no emptiness like the emptiness of the inability to receive, and no loss like the chronic, draining loss of the capacity to give and receive in empathy with others. There is no damage like the damage we do to ourselves in the stressful effort to escape our own lives. There is no sadness like the sadness of *It might have been.*

Only in making leisure and silence, safe time and safe space, can we begin to receive ourselves, and then to receive others. Only by risking the pain of bad feelings can we be open to our own inner world of feeling. Only by building relationships of trust, and by lingering in them long enough for our trust to deepen, can we begin, like beginning swimmers discovering water, to relax in the unknown element of our own feelings, and—albeit gradually —to make ourselves at home.

The Splitting of the Self

FIVE

Sometimes it all seems unreal and I feel like I'm not in my body.
You wouldn't say that if you knew the real me.
Somebody's always there inside my head, watching to see what will happen.
I think to myself, maybe I'll just split, man.

The self is always trying to survive. That is the first necessity, as it is for the body: to stay alive. To remain whole, to remain intact, comes second. We may give up an arm or a leg, a tooth or an eye; we may consent to be cut—in the belly, in the brain, in the heart—in order to keep ourselves alive and to live, as much as possible, without persistent pain.

For the self, survival means trying not to go crazy; and avoiding pain means trying to cut off feelings that we can't express or contain, feelings that threaten our sanity. As children, we learn how to survive in the world, which for children means the world of the family. In growing, and as adults, we continue to use these tactics for survival, and to weave them into strategies for coping with the total world of our interaction with others.

Each of us is a dancer who has learned to do only certain steps. As our spheres of action and awareness become more extended and various, they come to include not only the world of the family but the world of friends, the world of school, the world of work, the neighborhood, the society, and the entire condition of being an animal that changes, ages, and ultimately dies. We try to move to the music of each of these worlds; yet we try not to lose track of the rhythms and steps we know, the ones that first got us across the dance floor.

We all know dancers who can only do the box step, and people who, no matter what music is playing, only hear the waltz. For safety, we keep on doing what we know how to do. Although change and variation are more rewarding, they are also more difficult and more frightening. We change only with a feeling of wanting to dance another way, of wanting to step out of the box. We change only with a basic confidence that we can learn new steps without too much painful stumbling. Without that desire and that confidence, we remain locked into the box step, like a phonograph needle stuck in one groove, repeating the same tune.

Our patterns of defense are the box steps of our experience. They respond to the music of an inner track of feeling. This is the music of fantasy and nightmare, and of the haunting songs of childhood. It may be jangling and discordant, a tinkling music-box tune amplified until it blocks the senses. It may be showy and sentimental, but with an ominous undertone. Whatever it is, it is the music we heard when we first learned to dance, the life we knew when we first learned to live, the voices we first learned to recognize, the earliest rhythms, the scene that was, for us, the primal scene of human interaction. This music is composed, not of the overt sounds of ordinary life, but of the whispers in the inner ear.

Such whispers may be whispers of safety or of danger. There are people whose inner music murmurs a constant reassurance and stimulates free, spontaneous movements. But we are speaking here of dissonance that allows no resolution, and of rhythms that allow no alteration. Such compelling music comes to us like print-through on a tape recording, senseless and distracting. When we hear it, we begin to follow an old dance routine, moving in ways that are inappropriate to the present and that have little to do with the motions of those around us, even our partners. The phonograph needle has jumped into a well-worn, though hidden, track on the record of our experience.

Many of us live, at least part of the time, on a double track of experience and a double track of feeling. We are in the present, yet we also remain with the past. We live, or try to live, in the house of our present experience, yet we linger with other figures in remembered rooms, in the feelings of the childhood self.

We can detect this double track in a person when he reacts to a present situation in a way that is appropriate but excessive, with a super-charge of emotion. Sometimes, this might mean running away from a simple conflict situation, shaking with fear. This excess feeling is picked up from the past, from the inner track of early feeling and fantasy. Sometimes a person will explain quite rationally, *Well, I was angry at my child because this is what he did.* Then we learn that the parent's reaction to the child was a sudden, blind, uncontrollable rage. The child is bruised and frightened; and the parent is frightened, too, and asking, *How could I do that?* The answer probably lies somewhere in this person's own childhood, possibly in the rages of his own parent. If so, the phonograph needle has jumped onto the inner track, and the parent has reenacted the emotions of a *dance macabre.*

We are likely to be shocked at child abuse, and to view abusive parents as monsters, not as human beings who have themselves been bruised and abused. Of course children must be protected. But it is vital also to understand how and why such parents have tried to protect themselves in their own efforts to survive—and how people come to act from uncontrollable feeling, or to act seemingly *without* feeling.

Violence toward children and violence between adults are both more common than we might suppose. But these are only the overt expressions of a destructive, disintegrating process within the self. This process produces the even more common patterns of milder abuse and more subtle insult that plague families, from one generation to the next and the next, with the endless mirroring of bad experience. The parent who splits off feeling is like a broken mirror, giving back to the child a split image of the self.

What does this "splitting" mean? In today's vernacular, to "split" means to leave the scene, to pull out of the situation, to run away. As when a couple "splits up," it means to separate from something to which one was joined. A "split personality," on the other hand, is commonly understood to mean someone who is given to unpredictable shifts in his behavior— sometimes loving, sometimes hateful—as if containing two opposite "personalities" unknown to each other; in other words, the phrase "split personality" describes a person who is not well integrated, not joined within the self. When the loving person is there, the cruel, sarcastic, or violently raging one is unsuspected and forgotten; when the hateful one comes out, the loving or at least more moderate one has "split" and can't be found. The wife who is beaten at such times says *He becomes like another person.* The rejected boyfriend says *She cut me off like she didn't even know me.* The adolescent says of his mother, *It's no use trying to talk to her when she gets like that.* A wife says, *I talked to him about how I felt about my father's drinking, and he seemed so understanding. Then he taunted me about it when we quarreled.* These are descriptions of acts of splitting, of the cutting off of appropriate feeling.

THE SCHIZOID DEFENSE

The essence and purpose of splitting is to cut off feelings—and the perceptions that give rise to painful feelings. In this sense, we have already discussed splitting in the context of the manic patterns of defense. The person in the manic state has cut off any "bad" feelings of sadness, anger, and fright, and has censored out of consciousness any "bad" aspects of current reality; in other words, the person has split his own feelings and his own perceptions. Like our other defenses, splitting is protective and not necessarily destructive. But when individual acts of splitting become, in the process of growing, the person's habitual way of handling his feelings, they are rigidified into what we call the schizoid defense. When the schizoid defense is compulsive and pervasive in a person's emotional life, it destroys relationship to others and integration within the self. The person cannot connect himself with himself, let alone with others. When feeling is cut off, connection is broken and relationship is destroyed.

In some people, the personality is organized around the schizoid defense. In psychiatric terms, the "schizoid personality" means a person who is relatively divorced from his or her feelings and from relationships with others. This can be seen in the person's life style: He has few friends, none of them really close, and tends to isolate himself and to gain his satisfactions in fantasy and in solitary occupations. The person who is suffering a psychotic "schizophrenic reaction" is withdrawn within the self, cutting off appropriate feeling to a very marked degree; and he is split off, in his perceptions, from what we commonly consider the real world.

Acts of splitting may go even further in psychotic states, splitting the symbolic forms of the person's interaction. The usual, associative connections between thoughts and between words are loosened. In thinking and talking, the person goes off on tangents, fragmenting his perceptions, even at times fragmenting sentences and words in a desperate effort to protect the self from what is intolerable within the self and in the world. The reflecting glass and the observation window are both smashed in the effort to make their threatening images disappear.

Again, we are talking here about the most extreme forms of processes that may occur in any of us. As in thinking about the manic defense patterns and the manic state, we can look at these more frozen or more acute forms for illumination of what we ourselves may do more moderately. We are not attempting to categorize or to make a full or detailed delineation of psychic dynamics. Rather, we are concerned with sensitizing ourselves to the mechanisms by which all of us to some degree, and some of us to a very marked degree, handle our feelings, so that through awareness we may come closer to gaining the power to change where change is needed.

To understand acts of splitting as well as the more entrenched forms of the schizoid mechanism, we need to understand that we are talking about the handling of intolerable feeling and intolerable experience. By "intolerable" we mean that what happens to the person arouses so much fright and/or rage that the connection must be broken, like an electrical connection through which one is receiving a severe shock. The contact with the feeling must be cut off in order to protect the integrity of the self. The splitting, whether in the form of cutting off feeling or of fragmenting perception, is the person's way of confronting "crazy-making" experience without being made crazy.

SPLITTING IN CHILDHOOD

A child is hurt, and mother doesn't care, and the child knows she doesn't care. This feeling hurts so much that the child covers over the pain by withdrawing from the mother and refusing to feel toward her. The parents say loving words to a child, but the child perceives hostility in the father's voice or the mother's smile. This double message is very frightening, for it tells the child to do two opposite things: to come closer, yet to stay away, to feel safe and unguarded, and yet to be on guard. R. D. Laing has written extensively and eloquently about this interchange of subtle signals within a family, and about how the double message and the double bind necessitate the splitting of the self. The two opposite perceptions, the two opposite feelings, can't be taken in as an integrated form. They have to be split off from each other; and, since these are the experiences and feelings from which we construct a self, the self learns this process of splitting as the means of maintaining sanity.

A child develops a system of defenses that seems to help him to survive in his family-world. This system of defenses is closely related to what the parents can tolerate, as well as to their relationship with the child. Suppose the parents are people who depend heavily for their own sense of safety on an authoritarian role; in other words, they are made very uncomfortable by any disobedience—perhaps fearing they can't control the child and that chaos will result. The child of such parents may learn to rebel, cutting off his feelings for his parents so that he becomes armored against their rage; or he may learn to comply, cutting off his own independent action and desires.

Suppose there is severe conflict or even physical violence between the parents. This may be intolerably frightening to the child, and intolerably confusing. The child's sense of his need for both parents creates a rift within his own being which is the counterpart of the rift between the parents. To identify with father, as he must, to become a man, makes him, by extension, "bad" with relation to mother; to identify with mother, as he must, to have care, makes him bad to father. Many children try to escape this kind of conflict by tuning out the battle of the parents and by cutting off the fright caused by their violence, or by their violent wishes which are sensed by the child. Or the child may split off and deny his need for one of the parents, thus orphaning himself.

In other words, the child develops a facade, hiding his feelings even from himself, and perhaps displacing the fright onto strangers or dogs or wild animals. He dreams, not of his raging parents, but of monsters. In some families, the hostility between the parents is not acted out in violence, and may not be expressed in any overt form; yet it is still sensed by the child. The parents' secret hatred for each other becomes a secret the child also keeps, even from himself. But the anxiety it evokes makes the child afraid to be alone, or afraid to go to school.

The wounds of children often pass unnoticed. Parents, blinded by their own fright, often see a child as unconcerned when in fact the child has put up a facade, a smooth covering for an underworld of pain and terror. When parents become monsters in a child's eyes, or when the child's own feelings become wild forces beyond understanding or control, then the world becomes unbearable. This perception of the parents or of the self must be erased; the mirror must be smashed. The monsters must be disguised and put somewhere else, into a nightmare or a phobic zone.

When parents reject a child, either overtly or subtly, the child can view himself as bad, or he can view his parents as bad, or both. If the parents are felt as monsters, the need for their love and nurture must be denied. The child who feels she can't count on the help and support of a parent may cut off the awareness of her own needs and may develop an apparent premature independence which belies the need. Or, alternatively, the child may repeatedly split off and deny her sense of the parent as a monster. This perception becomes a well-kept secret, a skeleton in the psychic closet.

But the sense of the bad in the parent never loses its power; instead, it is split off and projected onto other figures who resemble and symbolize the parent. The rejected child, in his need for the parent, may prefer to view himself as the monster. This, too, is an insufferable perception that must be locked away in the basement. The child may become someone who can't admit to any mistake or fault, for to do so would confirm the sense of the self as bad. Instead the fault or weakness is split off and projected onto others; somebody else is always in the wrong.

A powerful by-product of such bad experience in childhood is an attitude of spite. Spite is a helpless child's reaction to feelings of betrayal, rejection, or injury. Spite works in the dark, as an attempt to punish or pay back others by damaging the self. Spiteful people spit out gifts or apologies, preferring revenge to repair. They may fall ill, eat poorly, spoil celebrations, fail in school or in careers, in delusional efforts to get back at others

The Splitting of the Self

by hurting the self, as if to say: *See what you made me do.* Although some forms of spite involve direct or indirect insults or acts against others, its dominant form is through self-injury designed to humiliate parents or mates. Alcoholics are masters of spite-work. The spiteful person is more *against* others than *for* the self; he is so involved in saying *No* to others that he ignores the cost to the self of the spiteful behavior.

The worst consequence of spite is that, although it begins with the feeling that bad others hurt the self, it develops into the feeling that the poison of spite makes the self bad, guilty of wishing harm to others, and finally, untouchable. Spite makes the self feel toxic; it makes the self an outcast. The punishing intention to *not enjoy* fixes the spiteful person in the position of saying *No, I won't, I don't need you.* Such attitudes are very costly; they result in the loss of love, gentleness, and pleasure. The only felt reality becomes revenge, and the person is locked in the delusion that refusing to feel anything for people is the way to gain superiority and power.

Whatever is split off in the self becomes inaccessible to growth. Acts of splitting isolate certain aspects of the self; and these aspects, then, cannot be modified or integrated into the total personality. Tender, vulnerable feelings, felt to be a source of pain because of repeated rebuffs, are locked away and cannot be used in relationship to others: This hampers the person's growth. Feelings of rage, felt to be dangerous or even murderous, are sealed in the boiler room, where they build up pressure but cannot be channeled into the normal aggression and self-assertion of daily life.

Development involves integration; and integration becomes impossible when acts of splitting are repeated so often, and prove so necessary a tactic for survival, that they take on the rigid, compulsive form of the schizoid defense. The feelings and perceptions that are locked out of the developmental process are locked *into* the forms and the intensity of childhood. The split self can't put its pieces together because they have jagged edges that have never been smoothed and re-formed in the growth process. The rage and fright and intense need that were too much for the child to handle and were thrust out of self-awareness retain their childhood power. The play goes on, but the monsters are always waiting in the wings.

THE SCHIZOID DEFENSE IN THE ADULT

This brings us back to our starting point, the double track of feeling and experience. The person who develops, in childhood, the patterns of the schizoid defense, has part of himself always in the past, locked into his destructive experience with the parent or another important person. As an adult, he tends to confuse events in the present with the events he could not assimilate in the past. A man in this position, while talking to his wife, may really be raging at his mother; in cutting off the wife, saying *I don't want to talk about it,* he uses the tactics he used with intrusive parents in order to avoid contact.

We are concerned here with the schizoid defense extended into adult life, as what we will call the schizoid mechanism. This is a basic repetition of a pattern or constellation in the person's original experience, a pattern which the person is always reproducing in his present life. A person may come to a counselor and say, *My boss is yelling at me and insulting me and humiliating me, and I can't say anything back to him, and my immediate supervisor is also persecuting me so I can't say anything to him, and I can't talk to my coworkers about it either.* Chances are that this person has reproduced, in his perceptions of the present, his original experience in the family. The monsters have been brought back onto the state to reenact the play of childhood—with the adult person acting out the role of helpless child.

A woman may come to a therapist and give long, detailed accounts of how badly she is treated by an unreasonable husband. She says, *He did this* and *He did that. He . . . . He . . . . He . . . .* She never notices her own provocations because she cannot conceive of herself as a separate person, performing actions that are separate from what her husband does. A woman in this emotional position feels that she is only half of a person, while her husband is her source of nurture and her lifeline.

Such a woman may be plagued by intense jealousy when her husband so much as looks at another woman. She may feel justified in this jealousy, taking the view that he is doing something disloyal if he feels attracted to someone else, even for a moment. But the intensity of her feeling, which is out of proportion to his actions, signals us that she has slipped over to the inner track of feeling, the track of the unconscious, split-off sense of being unloved. On the surface, she appears focused on the husband and his behavior. But she has really split from the present reality of her husband and what he actually does, careening off down the inner track of early experience, feeling that the husband's exclusive attention is her lifeline and his penis is the nurturing breast which is being pulled away. The woman's anxiety, in this situation, is not a realistic, limited concern about the attractiveness of a rival; it is a life-or-death anxiety, a childhood feeling masquerading as a socially acceptable, adult feeling of sexual jealousy.

It may be more or less realistic, of course, to fear the wandering of a particular mate's attention. But the difference between fear and anxiety is

The Splitting of the Self

that fear relates to reality problems and is more or less proportional to a given reality. Anxiety, on the other hand, is floating and protean, attaching itself to whatever situation is at hand. A person who suffers such anxiety about rejection and abandonment may be reassured about one situation only to start worrying about another. Fear is a response to an actual threat to the security of the self; but anxiety is always looking for an object or for an occasion in which to express itself. Anxiety relates to a continuous fantasy, a perpetual warning voice whispering in the inner ear of the self. Anxiety springs from the level of nightmare, from the level of split off childhood feeling and unassimilable experience.

A person may dream every night about a loss; and this may relate to a primary experience, such as the death of a parent early in the person's life or an early fear of abandonment. The person's unconscious life may be dominated by this hidden, split off, childhood fear of fatal loss, the loss of someone necessary to one's survival. Such a person may behave toward his children and his wife in a very controlling way. He may call the wife many times a day, always having to know her whereabouts. He may always be entering the children's rooms, or clutching them close even when, as adolescents, they want to pull away. Such a parent may become very upset when the child reaches an age to have friends and to go out at night; he may set unreasonable rules, or he may refuse to let the young person learn to drive. The refusal may be rationalized as *I won't let her do this because it's too dangerous.* But the real meaning of the refusal is *I won't let her go because separation means loss and loss means death.* The schizoid mechanism has switched this parent onto the inner track, the track of fantasy and nightmare, where the child is confused with another, earlier figure he feared to lose.

If a person is made to feel, in his original family situation, *I am murderous, I am jealous, I am raging,* the schizoid defense against these feelings may involve being sweet and all-giving, immersing oneself in a myth of family harmony which denies any bad feelings or any resentment. Such behavior may be adopted as a strategy against the dangerous, murderous fantasy which, it seems, would mean death to the parent and therefore death to the self. This way of handling aggressive, hostile feelings is then carried into adult life; the person tends to confront the world as a noncombatant, as a supplicant—unarmed and armless—unable to grasp for the self and ever dependent on "the kindness of strangers." Some independence may be developed in situations the person feels as safe. But often, when assertion is called for, the threat to the self is too great; it seems that to do for the self—to say *No,* or to demand attention to one's own need, or to press an issue—would be something bad and would bring on punishment. The schizoid mechanism switches the person back onto the inner track of anxiety; the fear of being bad makes the person afraid to act at all.

Aspects of the self or of the parents that are split off from a person's conscious awareness tend to be projected onto other people. The rage expressed and evoked by a controlling, overwhelming parent is projected onto a mate, a boss, or an authority figure of some kind; the murderous jealousy toward a brother or sister is projected, again, onto a mate, a friend, or a coworker. Such repetition of experience through projection doesn't happen by accident. A person who has split off unmanageable feelings and perceptions is always looking, on unconscious levels, for an opportunity to recover these aspects of the self. The person is always shopping for equivalents of the original family group. The woman who knew a raging father finds a husband who may appear very different, but who turns out to be the same—to do as her father did in important ways. The man whose mother "ran around" may consciously choose a wife who is above reproach, only to seek and find in her qualities resembling his mother's, or perhaps to drive her into the arms of other men.

Children can react to the monsters of their experience—the unmanageable forces—in one of three possible ways: with submissive surrender, cutting off the self; with over-aggression as a defensive response; or by making friends with the monsters by over-identifying with them. This last form of defense is what causes a person to say, *I couldn't stand my father, but I find myself acting like him; or, I'm getting more and more like my mother.* When a parent rages at a child, that parent is often reproducing the raging voice of his or her own parent, taken into the self. When experience with the parents is basically positive, the person is relatively free to choose, as he grows, what aspects of the parents he wants to take into the self, and in what ways he wants to depart from them. But when negative experience dominates the life of a child, it also dominates his adult life; the aspects of the parents that were intolerable to the child are split off from awareness, but can't be kept out of the territory of the self. The monsters in the parents invade the self, and remain as savages in the private wilderness of the self.

It is only through integration that we master ourselves and our experience. Murderous wishes and overwhelming fears can't be handled effectively by being split off from the conscious self. The monsters need to be domesticated in another way, through confronting and naming them, recognizing their origins, and setting limits to their power. When these tasks do not take place as the person grows, they often become the tasks of the corrective growth experience of psychotherapy. Otherwise, these untamed

The Splitting of the Self

forces of feeling continue to dominate the self. The energies of the self are devoted to keeping secrets, to hiding the fear and rage that could not be mastered in childhood. There is a secret group of persecutors, still performing their roles on the unconscious, inner stage, and being projected onto people in the world. There is a secret group of antipersecutory moves that have been developed to thwart these inner persecutors. Lying, dissimulation, defensiveness, self-sabotage, and the flattening of response are defensive moves designed to deal with this secret group. The person is always looking for opportunities to act out his contest with this original group of figures, and to triumph at last over these figures or their counterparts. The need to repeat and overcome the original intolerable experience becomes predominant over all other needs.

This means that the person who has split the self in self-defense has to keep on recreating the original situations where the acts of splitting began, as if the self were always trying to reintegrate; but he recreates these situations in ways that only confirm the need to split. If the person has an authoritarian, persecutory father, and then an authoritarian, persecuting boss, and an authoritarian, persecuting husband, and later an authoritarian, persecutory adolescent son, this person feels confirmed in her survival tactics. Such a person will not see that the men she chooses and her ways of treating them are designed to recreate the monster of early experience, and that the frustrations of her daily life are really recreations of the past.

Sometimes we see this repetitive pattern in an adolescent who finally reaches an age to leave his family, consisting of a passive father, an hysterical mother, and a provocative, acting-out sister, and moves out—only to take a room in a household consisting of a passive father, an hysterical mother, and an alcoholic son. The meaning of the schizoid mechanism is not *You can't go home again,* but *You can't leave home, wherever you go.* The scene changes, but the players projected on the secret stage of the self remain the same.

Sometimes we see such repetitions in someone who uses self-defeat as her form of the schizoid defense. The pattern of self-defeat is a paradox. Sometimes called "survival through negation," it consists of sabotaging oneself in order to avoid attack from the outside. The strategy of the self is to remain small, inconspicuous, unassertive, and unsuccessful in order to avoid the slings and arrows of envy, competition, and hostile assault. The message is: *I will do it to myself before you do it to me.* A classic story of such an attitude is about a person who has a flat tire on a country road and needs a jack in order to change the tire. He goes up to a nearby house, and on the way there he is saying to himself, *There won't be anybody home, and if there is anybody home, they won't want to lend me a jack anyway.* A person opens the door, and he says to this person, *You can keep your goddam jack.*

This is the schizoid mechanism at work. The person is always working on a fantasy that his needs will not be fulfilled. It doesn't matter what is happening in the present; it doesn't matter who opens the door or what that person is going to say in response. The person locked into the schizoid mechanism doesn't need anyone else to act out the play; he only needs a "straw person" who can be pushed, forced, and misperceived into conforming to the basic group of early figures.

People don't easily walk out on the action of the secret theater, even if the play is a flop. A woman with an alcoholic father who now finds herself with an alcoholic husband won't be quick to walk out on her marriage, nor is she even likely to demand that her husband change his ways. Why? Because her internal security depends, in a paradoxical way, on what is familiar, on the interruptions, craziness, and humiliations of the inner-track experience she had with the alcoholic father.

Even when a person begins to change and to do well in the present reality, there is a strong temptation to recreate the old, familiar play, like an old song one keeps humming in an absent-minded way, once one is reminded of it. For some people, anxiety rises whenever things begin to go well. Outer reality must then be made to conform to the reality of the inner track of feeling. On this inner track, the hidden, split-off portion of the self is struggling with old monsters. In order to maintain this hidden struggle, and yet to appear to be living in present reality, new monsters must be found to represent the old. The early, persecutory figure of a parent, grandparent, or sibling is represented by the new persecutory figure of a boss, a mate, a parent-in-law, or a child. The old fears of loss or damage to the self are represented by new anxieties.

These anxieties may be about a child, about money, about illness, about World War III breaking out, about crime in the streets, about a job, or about betrayal by one's wife or husband. There usually is some reality to which a given anxiety can be attached. But we can recognize the nature of this anxiety by its intensity; its disproportion; its persistence, and yet its floating, protean quality; and by the fact that somehow the person is not able to tackle the supposed reality problem in a realistic way. The person feels persecuted by her boss, but doesn't seek another job. The person worries about his health, but doesn't see a doctor. The person feels overwhelmed with money problems, but continues to run up bills. The person complains of bitter unhappiness in his marriage, but doesn't take steps to improve it or to end it. If these monsters of the present were to be overcome,

The Splitting of the Self

the person would have to create new ones, for their function is to validate the rage and panic that keep singing their persistent, strident notes on the inner track of the self.

When a person's emotional life is governed in this way by the schizoid mechanism, that person looks at reality through squinting eyes. The person has to avoid seeing others as they really are, and recognizing that others are real people, different from his projected images of old monsters. Just as the realities of the self are denied by the schizoid defense, the reality of others is also denied, because the self must remain committed to acting out its old dramas, in the service of its old, denied feelings. When the self is depersonalized, and intense feelings are split off from the conscious self, then others also cannot be seen as persons.

This is a basic and very difficult problem in marriage. Serious anxiety can be aroused in a marriage when one partner is locked into a schizoid box step and is trying to get his mate to do the same inappropriate dance. For example, a person locked into inner track feelings of being unloved will try to get his mate to confirm this old experience. The mate may start out saying, in various ways, *I love you.* The person locked into the schizoid mechanism will respond, in various ways, with messages like *You don't really love me, you only say you do. You're only trying to get something from me. You're only looking for a meal ticket/housekeeper. If you cared about me, you wouldn't have burned the dinner. How can you say you love me and still spend so much time at work? You love our new baby better than me. You spend more time with your friends than you do with me.* Or, *All right, you love me, but it won't last. You're looking for somebody else. All right, you love me, but you must be a jerk.*

These messages express a schizoid defense against the need to be loved. The defense becomes habitual out of bad experience—the terribly painful experience of not having what one needs—and it is carried into adult life to protect the self from pain. The closer the relationship the person is in, the more tempting it is to give up the defense and to open the self to feeling; at the same time, this arouses with ever more intensity the threat of being hurt again. The close relationship brings back the old pain, the old panic, the old fear of being swallowed up or of losing one's very life. The person switches onto the inner track where these fears are secretly humming, and performs the dance that seems to have saved him in the past, in which nobody comes too close or moves too far away.

The marital problems produced by this kind of mechanism are compounded when, as is often the case, *both* mates are involved in a schizoid box step. Then an elaborate set of complex, interlocking maneuvers are developed, in which reciprocal attack and anticipatory pushing-away are prominent moves. This kind of painful, compulsive dance can become so entrenched that it becomes a caricature of a mating ritual. If one partner tries to stop this kind of action, the pressure from the other to persist takes many forms, including threat and seduction. If one partner wants to leave the relationship, the reaction of the other may be *If you leave me I'll kill you,* or, *If you leave me I won't give you money, I'll fight you for the children, I'll ruin your life.* Again, this reaction comes from the inner track, the track of life-and-death anxiety. The track of *Kill or be killed,* the track of *Separation means death.* Here, again, are the blind, early terrors about survival, and the compulsive moves developed in order to survive.

People in this kind of interaction can't see each other any better than they can see themselves. The schizoid mechanism interferes seriously with the capacity to look at another person and to see that person clearly. Sometimes a couple will come to a marriage counselor and show in very concrete ways that they don't see or hear each other. They sit in the room and don't look at each other. They talk, not to each other, but to the counselor *about* each other, as if the counselor were a judge or a parent. When they do talk to each other they don't hear each other accurately, but with a kind of auditory hysteria. As they talk, they express bizarre distortions of who the other person is; and when they begin to deal with the reality of the other person, they say, *I don't believe it.* If a husband says to his wife, *The reason I've been avoiding you and clamming up for the past 17 years is that you attack me and I'm afraid of you,* the wife will say, *I can't believe this. This is unreal.* For the wife has been busy, perhaps, projecting her callous, indifferent father onto her husband, absolutely unable to see the husband clearly or to see that he is frightened. The wife's demand for an ideal nurturing father blinds her to the reality of her husband. She is trapped on the track of "betrayed victim."

People often fail to perceive each other's frailty and each other's feelings of fright, pain, and weakness because they have had to split off such feelings in themselves and cannot risk the disarming effects of awareness. Instead, they maintain a projected image, a fantasy of the other as a persecutor, modelled upon a persecutory figure in the past. Of course a persecutor cannot have fears or feelings. Rather, the persecutor must be seen as the bad one, the source of all trouble and unhappiness, the originator of rage, the repository of blame, the domestic monster. The persecutor must be seen as holding all the power, and therefore all the responsibility in a relationship, while the self remains the helpless victim or the defiant rebel who continually "splits" from involvement in order to survive.

Such a pattern often operates between husband and wife, and equally often between parents and adolescent children, with each seeing the other in the monstrous frame of childhood. Again, the real feelings of the self and the reality of the other are split off from awareness. The need, the fright, and the rage in the self are relegated to a back room in the life space of the self; but this back room turns out to be the control room, the projection room of the secret theater.

The problem with the schizoid mechanism as a dance-master or director of the secret theater is that all the scripts and dances lead to the same emotional dead end: denial of the bad in the self, scapegoating, self-betrayal, confusion of self and other. Whatever the form of the schizoid mechanism, it remains impermeable to experience, a rigid barrier to learning from experience. Like a myth or an ideal, the schizoid mechanism destroys information that does not conform to its own pattern. A person trapped in the schizoid mechanism denies bad feeling in the self but feels that he or she is *so* bad that self-identity is distorted. The person in the schizoid mechanism is unable to say or feel *I feel bad,* or *I'm sorry I made that mistake* because of the barrier of denial, splitting, and projection that puts the bad outside the self.

For women, one dominant form of the schizoid mechanism is the pattern: nurse/victim/savior. Whatever situation such a woman finds herself in, she bends it so that she is able to cling to the role of passive victim or omnipotent helper. Overt aggression and conflict are taboo. Conflict avoidance restricts learning and prevents acceptance of the active and sexual aspects of selfhood. The nurse/victim can never be wrong or bad—and cannot grow into an adult. She makes the ideal martyred wife for an alcoholic.

For men, a dominant form of the schizoid mechanism is the Faustian pattern of constant competitive activity, with devaluation of any receptivity or relaxation. Don Juan is a variant of this pattern. The future is always idealized, the present rushed, and the past never considered. Such a person envies others, greedily devours experience, and appreciates nothing. Such a person is also unable to understand or to learn from the damage and cost of exploitive behavior. To such a person, only competition, winning, and controlling the future is important.

All the forms of the schizoid mechanism tend to be rigid and righteous, inflexibly repetitive. All these patterns involve violating others in the service of the need to be good or to be in control, and to be invulnerable to the suffering of childhood. The impenetrable armor of the schizoid defense protects the self against being betrayed, at the cost of betraying the human potential in the self and in others. Whether a person's pattern is the Big No of spite, the Faustian arms-race, the Big Nurse, or some other form of schizoid non-involvement, the self continues to be withheld, and at the same time remains, in secret, untouchably toxic.

Whatever form the schizoid mechanism takes, it is composed partially of moves the parents made and partially of the child's countermoves to those moves—all unconsciously programmed. Such prescribed moves divide the self because the child's effort, both to hold onto the parents and to reject and punish them, obscures the limits of the self, and interferes with being *for the self* as a separate being. Instead, the person is always busy being with the parents or against the parents. Feeling safe means being for the self—not clinging to others, not spiting them, not devoting the energies of the self to competition regardless of its cost.

People in the grip of the schizoid mechanism say odd things: They say, *You don't trust me*—meaning, *I don't trust you,* and, perhaps, *I can't trust anyone.* They say, *Stop attacking me,* while provoking more attacks; and *You never listen,* while remaining unable to open their own ears. They say, *You don't give me anything, you only take from me*—meaning, *I can't give to you because I've never had enough for myself.* They say, *You're killing me*—meaning, *I'd like to kill you;* and they say, *I'd like to kill you*—meaning, *I can't survive without your love.* In the schizoid world, need is confused with rage; and the self is confused with the other, reality with fantasy, and the present with the past.

The person entrenched in the schizoid defense is at once locked in and locked out: locked into the embattled world of the child, where he first learned to survive by splitting the self; and locked out of the arena of reality, where in the successive contests of development he could do real battle with his personal demons. Such a person is locked into a destructive, fantasy interaction with others; and he is locked out of the richness of real involvement. The schizoid mechanism is like a buzz saw, separating the person from his real feelings and from his real, present experience; and at the same time it is like an instant zipper, an infernal machine encasing him in "his bag" of habitual distortions and anachronistic fears. At once victim and persecutor, the person is compelled to do a repetitive re-enactment of an early nightmare.

There is a way out of this nightmare. As always, the way out is the way into the self, into involvement with others, and into the closed-off, boarded-up, condemned rooms of emotional experience. These are the rooms split off from the house of the self: the space of trust, the space of intimacy, the space of true involvement, the space of empathy and love. The person who lives by the schizoid defense needs help to enter these rooms, for, in the world of his experience and therefore of his persistent fantasy, these are the rooms where monsters lie in wait, ready to devour him with their possessiveness, to disintegrate him with their rage, to make him crazy with their own changing faces and split identities, to annihilate him with their overwhelming power. These are the rooms—the spaces of empathy and trust—that have proved so threatening that they have become forbidden areas, phobic zones in the life of the self.

The help needed is that of a trusted other person, often a psychotherapist, who knows the names and the shapes of monsters, and who can stand with the person and look his monsters in the eye without turning to stone, without experiencing the frozen terror of the person estranged from feeling and therefore from his own life. A person is needed who can dare to look at what is split off from the self—one who can accept the projections of split-off feeling without confirming them, and who can give these projections back to the person with their true names. Someone is needed who can walk with the person into the haunted crazy-house of the self, one who can help him to look at the ghosts and monsters without screaming, one who can help him to look into the funhouse mirrors without having to destroy his reflections by shattering them to bits. Someone is needed to provide the safe space and the safe time of a corrective relationship, a place to put the parts of the self together again, and to re-know them as a whole—that is, to remember and recognize the self. That is a long and sometimes terrifying effort; but through it the splits in the self can be repaired, and unsafe space can be cleared and made safe again.

Making the Self: Separation and Integration

SIX

> *I got to get myself together, man.*
> *It's like there was always somebody watching over me. I guess it's time to cut the apron strings.*
> *I dreamed I was holding onto his hands and I said, But I can't let go, I'll die.*
> *I can't live without her.*

Making the self is a process that never ends until life itself ends. The house of the self is not static but organic, expanding or contracting in response to the inner and outer climate, always growing and always dying. We long for time in the sun; and we tend to remember the past or look to the future in some idealized form, as if there were really such a thing, in our life as human beings, as permanently safe space or totally safe time—in which we had or will have all we want and all we need.

The child looks at adults and longs to enter the adult world and escape the constraints of childhood. The adult falsely remembers childhood as carefree. The adolescent looks to his own adulthood as an ascent to power, in which he will exercise simple wisdom to correct the folly of his parents. The middle-aged adult looks to youth, forgetting its pangs and confusions, and longs to be young again. Each sibling envies the privileged life space of the other; and each sex, at times, envies the other's sexual and social being. Even death is idealized by the religious as the gateway to a heaven that will compensate us for all the pains of this world. It seems that life should—somehow, somewhere, sometime—offer us a clear path to the fulfillment of all its promise.

Making the Self: Separation and Integration 79

But of course we know that isn't how life is. Our terrain is at best uneven, and at worst a landscape of deserts and abysses, spaces and times to be lived through in anxiety and deprivation. How much of life is like this, and how we traverse such difficult spaces in our experience, depends largely on how fully we have accomplished the earlier, equally difficult tasks of growth.

We can see the work of childhood as a two-fold, yet single task: the *separation and integration* of the self. As we grow, this task changes its context and its forms, but in its essence it remains the same. We move through many stages of development in evolving from the infant, just out of the mother's body and still clinging to her breast, into the relatively autonomous, relatively whole adult self. But we remain involved, throughout our lives, with the issue of what it is to be a separate self, and what it is to be whole. Separation is a constant effort, and integration a constant process. We call them a single task because we can't put ourselves together without, at the same time, separating ourselves from others and from our own fantasies. And, on the other hand, we can't separate ourselves without making a self that is "together" enough to manage life on its own.

We are able to leave the safety of the mother's body, the early embraces, and the early forms of relationship, only as we are able to carry safety within ourselves. We are able to outgrow the needs of childhood only as we are able to gain fulfillment for ourselves. The capacity to fulfill our needs includes being able to feed ourselves in every sense, to take what we need from others, and to give what we need to give in relationships in order to offer satisfaction to others and to express themselves. We are able to grow beyond the structuring of childhood only as we can structure, process, and utilize experience for ourselves. In growing, we have to learn both to take in and to screen out experience, to give and to withhold, and to utilize what we give and take in order to maintain ourselves as separate, yet connected beings—open to experience, yet not flooded by it; and related to others, yet not clinging to others as the source of life itself.

MAKING THE SELF IN CHILDHOOD

In the beginning, of course, we must cling and be fed in order to survive. We are dropped from the safe space of the womb into a life space that is unsafe. The infant human being can easily die—of cold, of hunger, of blows, of disease, of unknown causes, of the lack of a mothering figure to offer stimulation, nurture, and the rhythmic return of a familiar face, voice, and touch, offering a predictable response to the rhythms of bodily need. For the infant, *Separation means death* is not a fantasy but a reality.

To make safe space of the new, supremely dangerous world outside the womb, we need to develop a map and a clock—a sense of space and a sense of time. The original map is the map of the infant's own body, at first continuous with the mother's. The original clock measures time by the ebb and flow of bodily need and response. We need to discover, as organisms, that this ebb and flow is predictable and secure, that our hunger will be fed, our discomfort eased, and our crying soothed. We need to learn about our own bodies as tolerable inhabitable space that is not flooded with stimuli of annihilating intensity—neither the stimuli of sound and light bombarding us from outside nor the agonizing inner signals of unsatisfied need.

As infants, we have few needs; but they are intense, and their satisfaction is vital to survival as well as to the development of what Erik Erikson calls basic trust. As infants, we make a continual, pressing demand upon our caretakers, not only to provide nurture and comfort, stimulation and respite, but to provide them in finely attuned response to our individual rhythms. The *mutuality* of this process is also vital. The infant has to learn, in the act of feeding, not only that the milk is available to satisfy his hunger, but also that it is regulated through his own efforts—that his sucking and his signals of hunger and satiation gain the finely attuned response of the mothering person.

Our first problem of integration is the integration of what our senses tell us. Our intelligence is grounded in our sensorimotor system, which responds to the holding, touching, breathing, and grasping of our mothers and fathers. Our mind is first in our skin, and in our being "minded." Our first social "group" is the unity of self and mother. The mother's look, the mother's touch, and the mother's embrace make our original life space and tell us of our value and whether we can trust the world of others and the inner world of our own strivings. Our first learning of trust is in this pairing, this relation with the human being who gives us, not only care and nurture, but the first experience of giving and receiving. The luckiest infants are those for whom this process is mutually gratifying—to the infant and to the nurturer—for this is the basis of all relationships with other human beings.

As the infant grows into the child, he becomes increasingly better able to tolerate breaches in closeness to the nurturing person, and minor frustration of his needs from time to time. In other words, safe space is expanded as we grow, widening in a circle ever more extended from the presence of the mother. And safe time is also extended—time during which the child can bear not to be fed, not to be held, and not to have the stimulation of company. Or, on the other hand, time during which the child can bear to be with other people and can mobilize the self to respond to them is also extended. We learn to tolerate longer periods between feedings, longer periods of play and of sleep; we learn to be alone sometimes and yet to feel safe and held; and we learn to be with other nurturing people besides the mother, and to overcome anxiety about strangers.

WHAT IS NEEDED TO MAKE THE SELF?

All of these developments are lengthy and complex; and it is not our purpose here to retrace them in all their complexity and detail, as various writers on child development have already definitively done. Rather, our purpose is to understand what enables the child to separate and integrate himself. It is a vital function of the pair relationship with the mothering person to provide a model and a context for this pulling away and gathering together of the self. Ideally, the relationship with the "motherer" offers safe time, in which the infant is not rushed beyond her capacities into the achievements of more advanced stages of growth; and it also offers safe space, the embrace which remains as a refuge to the infant and to the growing child, from which he can venture in development, and to which he can periodically return to seek comfort and sustenance for the ever more difficult tasks of growth.

The mother's embrace feels safe to the child insofar as it is responsive to the child's needs. This means, first of all, that the mother must be reliably *there* for the child, until, through graduated experiences of separation, his safe space for venturing away from the mother, and his safe time for doing without the mother, are extended and increased. It means, too, that the mothering embrace, while secure, mustn't be confining—that it mustn't become "smother love" in which the growing person is held too long and too closely in order to serve the needs and anxieties of the mother at the expense of the child's growing.

This is a delicate balance of forces, as is the mutual process of feeding and being nurtured. The nurturer of someone's growth has the task of offering enough closeness, yet not too much; enough separation, yet not too much or too soon. The ideal parent is there or not there according to the needs and rhythms of the child. But of course no parent is ideal; and an "ideal" parent, for that matter, wouldn't really be ideal, for the child would learn too little of mutuality, of tolerating frustration, and of accommodating to the rhythms of others.

What is needed, then, is a long, graduated series of experiences in which the child learns to be separate and yet to feel safe in his separateness. His safety, first known inside the mother's body, is found in her arms, and then in the arms of other mothering and fathering figures; it is found in the close, warm space of the sheltering blanket and the bassinet, then in the crib, and then in his own bed and in his own room. The safe place, at first meaning *Where mother is,* becomes also *Where father is,* and then generally, *Where a familiar person is there to hold me.* The safe world, at first meaning *Home,* is extended to mean *Home, and other known places away from home, where there are people I can trust.*

The sense of safety and of trust means, most basically, the feeling *I will be fed,* which in turn means, in its most extended sense, *I will have what I need.* For the child, this means mostly, at first, *I will have what my body needs:* food, rest, elimination, cleansing, stimulation, and protection. These meanings are of course never lost, even in our lives as adults; but they are constantly developed and refined into needs that are felt in more complex and more variegated ways. The sleep of the infant means the satisfaction of being filled and it means respite from stimulation both from outside and from the stirrings of inner needs. The sleep of the adult has the same meanings and the same preconditions, but in a more complex and extended form: The adult person rests poorly or well according to how well he has been able to satisy his needs for food, for elimination, for sexual expression; and also for emotional expression, for mental activity, and for empathetic response from others. The infant whose stomach is not well filled or is over-filled may be awakened by the pangs of hunger or indigestion. The child or the adult may be disturbed by these same signals, and also by other signals of being ill "fed" in different ways—in other words, by the stirrings of anxiety, loneliness, and terror. The infant may be startled out of sleep by loud sounds or sudden light; the child or adult may suffer from these stimuli, and also from more personal and less concrete invasions, such as memories of the day or images of other people transformed into nightmare figures.

For the child, then, as he or she evolves from an infant into an adult, these meanings of *safety* and *fulfillment* become more complex, while never losing their basis in the body, and their bodily expressions. But this is not the most significant change in the meaning of *safety* to the child as he grows. Underlying this elaboration of need, fulfillment, and response is something far more vital: the development of the infant into a separate person.

The fetus has its life within the mother, and the infant has his life in her nurturing. But every fetus is on its way to becoming an infant, and every infant is already, at birth, evolving into a wholly separate being. If safety means, for the infant, *I will be fed* and *I will be given what I need,* it also means, from the first days of life, *I will feed, I will take my food, I will strive for what I need and take it into myself.* The infant, in other words, is

Making the Self: Separation and Integration

not passive, and the receiving of the infant is as active a process as the giving of the mothering person. This is what is meant by Bettelheim's concept of *mutuality* between infant and mother. We learn our separateness from our efforts and their results. We learn from our own activity and the responses it evokes to conceive of the self as separate from mother, and to believe in the possibility of survival as a separate self.

Of course this process is not intellectualized, but is experienced in the body. The infant cries, and mother comes: *My crying brings food.* Or, mother doesn't come: *Mother is separate from myself and may come or not.* If mother stays away, or chronically comes too late, when the infant is already suffused with the pain of his need, it seems to mean: *My crying is no use.* The infant may withdraw into his own emptiness. If the infant sucks at the breast and gets enough milk, it means: *My sucking gets food.* If there is not enough milk, it may mean to one infant: *I must cry some more, and more vigorously.* Another, repeatedly discouraged, may learn: *There is never enough food for my needs.*

These statements are absurd, of course, because these experiences come before speech and concept, before words can order thought and interpret feeling. But, by thinking of infantile experience in these simple and perhaps over-simplified terms, we can surmise something of how personality and expectation are formed in the very beginnings of the self. For the crucial relation between *I am fed* and *I feed* continues to operate throughout our lives. Our needs are elaborated, and our activity changes its forms and its specific meanings; but the conviction, *I will get my food,* which becomes finally, *I will get food for myself,* remains as the basis for our separateness. The infant or child that learns *I can't get enough food for myself* or *I can't get what I need by my own strivings* learns that he dare not go beyond the circle of the mother's care; in fantasy, he remains in the body of the mother, refusing to be born.

We can project the meaning of such experience from infancy through childhood and into adulthood, for we all carry in ourselves the infants and children we were; and we are all, in a sense, striving to milk the breast of our daily reality. Whether the milk flows readily from a particular breast (or life situation) is one element in our satisfaction with the feeding. Literal starvation would bring out the desperate infant in any one of us, and at any stage of life. Similarly, the real conditions of any life may be, at a given time, too much to bear, and may drive us back into a childlike dependency as we find it impossible to satisfy our own needs.

But our experience of ourselves as feeders, and of the process of feeding, especially as we learn it in infancy and childhood, remains an equally vital factor in our lives. Our skill in feeding, our ability to cope with frustration, to wait, to increase our efforts, to rest and strive again, to employ our aggression in useful ways to bring forth food or other fulfillment; our confidence to leave the dry breast and seek another, more promising source; our expectation of finally, somehow, obtaining the milk that will be adequate to our needs—these factors decide what happens when the breast of our reality runs dry. The sense of the self as actively receiving food and giving forth the products of the body and of the self remains at the heart of the capacity to separate, which is essentially the belief that one can live outside the mother's body, and outside the womb of her care and influence.

Of course there is much more to infantile experience; and it should be clear, too, that we are speaking here not only of an infant feeding, but of the entire process of nurturing a child. The eyes, the touch, and the tone of voice of the parent are part of this nurturing. The nurturing process, like the child's needs, is elaborated over time; and not only does the actual food become more varied, but *what* and *how much* and *when* and *how* the child needs to receive from the parent is always changing and has its own ebb and flow. The constant element in this process is the striving of the growing person to achieve a separate, integrated self. The constant condition of this process is the presence of the parent when and as it is needed: to nurture, to structure, to offer help and protection, to set limits—all in the service of the development of the child as a separate self.

We tend to describe child development in terms of its ideal norms, and to speak of growth in terms of how it might ideally take place. But, as in Plato's cave, we see in the real-life process of growing only, at best, the reflections of ideal forms. All life is a stressful, albeit fruitful effort; all growth is uneven and marred by misfortune; all parents are human beings with their own needs and their human errors; all children are flawed and to some degree deprived, when seen in terms of an ideal. What we hope for is that growth may be relatively successful; that life may offer "our share" of happiness; and that growing children may evolve into relatively mature, integrated, separate yet relating persons. We need to remember all that can go wrong in the growth process in order to be free to look fearlessly for the sources of our own troubles. To do so is to blame neither our parents nor ourselves, for all human efforts fall short of what we can conceive that they could be. But we still can seek the happiness of a persistent striving for what we think life could be; and we can work for a persistent reprocessing and recreation of our experience in the light of a new comprehension.

SEPARATION ANXIETY

What can go wrong, then, in the growth of a child? We have spoken already of "separation anxiety" and of the meaning of separation for the infant. When we see young children who can't leave the mother's side, older children who can't go to school, adolescents who become withdrawn and won't leave the house, or young adults who can't leave home—we are looking at separation anxiety, the feeling of a growing person that he or she can't leave the mother and survive.

Separation anxiety doesn't come from a child's being "spoiled"—although the lack of experiencing separation in graduated forms, by being away from mother for short periods, may certainly contribute to its outbreak. But, in general, children are not "spoiled" by attention to their needs, only by overattention to their wants. Separation anxiety, or the persisting need for the mother, beyond the usual age, comes about rather because of some lack or abrupt breach in the attachment to the mother, or because of a smothering quality to the mother's attention. The more stable and predictable, the more accessible and responsive the mothering person has been, the less anxious the child will tend to be when separations occur. A child who feels secure in the relation with the mother goes into the world with the feeling that, whatever happens, he will be able to get his food and fulfill his needs. But the child who has experienced his mother as unreliable, perhaps because of a sudden absence at the wrong time in his development, may feel unsure. He may feel, *Maybe the food won't be there after all. Maybe, if I venture away from mother, I'll never find her again.*

The child's emotional life has one simple and solemn theme: his need for closeness to the mother and his anxious fantasy that all separation implies losing the mother, the source of nurture, forever—in other words, that *separation means death.* A strong counter-theme, of course, is the striving to grow and therefore to separate, and to constantly extend the radius of safe space beyond the original circle of the mother's care. Much of our growing can be seen as the weaving together of these themes, and their development into an integrated pattern of interdependence with other human beings. But, as we grow, there is an ebb and flow, with sometimes the fear of separation, and sometimes the urge to separate, taking the predominant role. We long to remain in the womb, yet we strive to escape its confines.

This is part of the meaning of safe space and safe time in the original relation with the mothering figure. The child needs to have time to go away and come back to the mother, and to have her leave and return, with the interval of separation at first brief, and then ever more extended. There need to be many departures and many predictable reunions, so that the child gradually increases his tolerance of separation, just as he gradually extends his attention span and his entire perspective on time and space. In the beginning, an hour can be an abyss, an eternity; and out of sight means, not out of mind, but out of the world.

THE UNSEPARATED SELF

What does all this mean in adult life? A traumatic or chronic separation that is "too much, too soon" is a bitter loss, a source of bad expectations in any relationship, and a serious hindrance to developing an integrated, separate self. The infant who feels, *I can never get enough food,* and the child who feels, *No one is there for me to trust* becomes an adult who suffers spells of anxiety and depression, especially in situations reminiscent of the early threat of loss. A woman may suffer a severe depression when her own baby is born and leaves her empty, or when her own child goes to kindergarten. Or she may feel the same way if her husband goes on a long business trip, or if the family moves to the suburbs, leaving her old neighborhood. A person may suffer anxiety whenever he or she is alone, reexperiencing the feelings of childhood. A man who has lost his job may feel, not only the reality concern—the loss of money and status, the appropriate anxiety—but also the deep, intolerable terror of the child who feels loss is death and absence is a desert in which he can never find food again.

The adult who has suffered traumatic loss, or the threat of loss, early in life always carries within himself the anxious, clinging child—the child who grieves for the mother or who rages at her absence, the child who cannot trust, the child who wants to punish others for his pain, the child who feels his very survival is at risk. The feelings of such a child are a major cause of what we have called the schizoid defense, the splitting of the self. Some children can't bear their panic, their pain, or their despair, whether it concerns the loss of the mother, the lack of good mothering, the fear of being abandoned, or the loss or lack of the mother's love. Some children can't bear the violence of their parents, their hostility toward each other, or their unresponsiveness to the needs of the child. Some children can't bear the smothering effect of being overfed, overprotected, overattended, dominated, and possessed by the mother—as if they were a part of the mother's body, and not separate beings in their own right. They are always watching themselves, or feeling watched—always listening to inner voices not their own. To avoid the unbearable, they "split," cutting off feeling within themselves; and then they remain split, unable to "get together" a self which is integrated enough to enjoy the world.

To see overmothering or overprotection as a problem may seem like a contradiction to what we have said about separation anxiety. The deprivation inherent in "smother love" is a paradox and must be understood as such, for it is a major cause of splitting and can be more damaging than the partial deprivation of maternal attention. The reason for this is that the overprotective, overinvolved mother also conveys the message *Separation means death.* This message is conveyed to the child, not through neglect or abandonment, but through the separation anxiety of the mother, who is overprotective and overattentive precisely because she herself fears separation—both for herself and for the child—and because she often fears her own underlying hostility toward the child.

The child also learns *Separation means death* from this mother in another way: In attempting to grow away from the mother, as he must to become an adult, he encounters her anxiety and rage. The message he receives is not *I may leave you and you will die*— the message of the neglectful parent—or *I may kill you,* which is the fantasy message of the abusive or hostile parent. Instead, the message of the over-close, overattentive, overinvolved parent is *If you leave me by becoming a self, you will die and you will also kill me, because you are a part of me, you are my food.* This message sounds terrifying when stated this way; and it is no less terrifying to the child, who can't grow without splitting the self, who can't separate from mother, and who can't take in and integrate what he perceives in his relation to the mother. The kind of fright that is produced by these feelings binds the child to the parent all the more strongly because the bond is ambivalent. The young person can't become a self because he remains partially glued, like a Siamese twin, to the original pair bond. If he should succeed in partially separating himself, there is so much pain, terror, and conflict in the process that any close relationship revives the fright of the first relationship: that he will be swallowed, smothered, kept from being a self, locked in. At the same time, the fear of not being able to survive on his own may produce an anxious clinging that in fact will tend to drive others away, so that his fear of being rejected for being himself, of being abandoned and locked out, is readily confirmed. The person who has been treated as part of the mother, someone not entitled to be a self, tends to remain a partial self, feeling his survival to be at risk whether he is in or out of a relationship. The person who has had "too much mother," as well as the person who hasn't had enough, feels in danger wherever he goes.

THE VIABLE SELF

Then what does it mean for growth to go well, and what is it to make a viable self? We have spoken a great deal about separation and about the capacity to become a separate self. We know that capacity is based upon the confiction: *I can take in what I need, wherever I go.* We know that this conviction, in turn, is based upon good feeding and good experience with the original mothering figure and the original family group.

What separation really means, then, is being able to take in enough food, enough love, enough structure, and enough good experience to be able to let go of their original sources and still survive and grow. The person who can separate has taken in, from the mother and other nurturing figures, what is needed for the self. These original good figures are securely installed within the safe house of the self; they are transformed into the capacities of the self to give and receive what is needed—food, love, stimulation, and rest—with a sense of the boundaries of the self and of others, of the proportions of need and satisfaction, and of the limits of reality and of fantasy. These capacities are formed in the self through the rhythmic processes of giving and receiving, filling and emptying, separating and joining, that are experienced with the mothering figures and are integrated with one's own bodily rhythms. These processes become the rhythms and functions of the mature self; they mark the time of our original clock, and they define the spaces of our original map of safe and unsafe space.

This is the sense in which separation and integration are themselves a single continuous process. We leave the breast only as we are able to feed ourselves; and we are able to feed ourselves only by letting go of the magic breast. We are able to let go of any specific source of good only as we are able to find and make other sources for our food; and we are able to seek other sources only by learning to feed for ourselves while still at the breast, and then in the highchair, and then at the family table—by learning to take over more and more of the feeding process.

The same is true of the process of moving about and exploring the world, the communication process, the learning process, and the processes of emotional giving and receiving. We learn to walk only as we can leave the mother's side; and we can leave her side only as we are able to learn to creep, to crawl, to walk, to discriminate between safety and danger, to choose a direction. We explore the world only from a place of safety; and we extend the boundaries of our safety only through exploration. We relate to others only as we are able to leave the original family; and we are able to leave the original family only as we are able to integrate good ways of giving and receiving and to carry these processes beyond the family and into our other relationships. We learn to select, from our native repertoire of sounds, the words that the family recognizes as meaningful; we are able to move out, talk with others, and learn new words and new thoughts only by integrating and using the family language; and the family language becomes meaningful only as it comes to be used in the world, without which the family would need no elaboration of its language. We can think and feel as ourselves only insofar as we become separate; we can separate ourselves only insofar as we can take in the feelings, concepts, and rhythmic experiences that are the stuff of which the self is made.

Making the Self: Separation and Integration

The self is in the making every day, and especially in the days of childhood—pulling away from others and pulling together the self, separating from others and joining the self together, drawing into the self what can be utilized for growth and pushing out what is useless, excreted, outgrown, inimical. To make the self requires, every day, at every state of growing, the space and time that are safe for these processes—the safe space and safe time made for the self by nurturing, sheltering human beings—in the ebb and flow of relationship, of giving and receiving, and of separation and integration.

Basically, integration means drawing together to form a whole, and holding together as a whole. This is what we mean when we speak of an integrated self, in contrast to a split or partialized self. The split self is split because of messages and experiences that couldn't be "put together." It is split because of pain and terror that couldn't be incorporated into a whole self because they might destroy that whole. When a person says of an experience, *I was destroyed* or *I just fell apart*, the person is usually describing a brief disintegration under some temporary but overwhelming stress. "Splitting," or what we have called the schizoid defense and the schizoid mechanism, is the more lasting or more compulsive form of such disintegration, under the force of more chronic stress. Severe stress, or an unhappy combination of stresses at a given time, is always a threat to our integration—in proportion to its severity and to the number of stresses that coincide. The effects of such stress depend upon the degree to which a person has been able to build an integrated self. For some people, the psychic structure breaks down when a stress in the present is laid upon a "fault" in the foundation, opening a great crack in the construct of the self. For the self is a continuous construct, whose foundation is the integration of childhood. The foundation is more or less firm or faulted, more or less resilient or rigid, more or less strong or frail, and more or less vulnerable—at different points—to the stresses imposed on the self in the course of the life cycle.

When a person is not able to achieve a well integrated self, there is a feeling of not knowing who he is or where he stands. This is another way of saying that it's hard to tell where the person's boundaries are. The person may show sudden, unpredictable shifts in his behavior and become "a different person," as we discussed in the chapter on splitting. The person may find it hard to come to a decision, and he may be constantly shifting his opinions. The person may run out on his major or minor commitments, giving others a feeling that he can't be counted upon; and he may also feel that he can't count on himself, for he doesn't know how he's going to feel about something from one day to the next. The person may construct an elaborate structure of behavior patterns—around family, work, social relationships, and leisure activities—and yet he may feel that he is only going through the motions, that it isn't really he who is living his life, and that he and his life are really empty inside.

The feeling of emptiness in the poorly integrated self makes the person very vulnerable. The poorly integrated self, of course, has been unable to separate, to pull away from the parents. The person may have left his parents in a physical or geographic sense; but he may actually carry one or both of them with him and he may always be looking for someone on whom to lay their images. As the person remains partially fused with the parent, the tendency is to fuse with any other person who comes close, as if that person were also the parent. The person may make, or try to make, a friendship in which neither person is allowed to have any other friend, or to make any move in life without the other feeling threatened and abandoned. The person may cling to a lover or mate as if that other person were the source of his very life. The person will cling to a child as if the child were part of himself, and he will be unable to let that child separate and integrate as a separate person with his own needs and his own life.

Such a person is clinging inside the self to an idealized parental figure who is confused with food, and, on the other hand, to a devaluated figure who is confused with a garbage pail and is used as a dumping ground for rage. Both of these figures, represented by the same other person with whom this person happens to be in a relationship, are held onto with great intensity. This is the meaning of the severely ambivalent or hostile-dependent relationships we sometimes see in practice—the unhappy love affiars or the "negative symbiotic" marriages that may last for many years, with each partner torturing the other and yet remaining glued each to the other. The process of clinging to these figures—the nurturing figure and the "garbage" figure—uses up the energy that the person would need for integration. Instead of integrating the self, the person integrates a conglomerate unit. An enormous amount of time and energy goes into attempting to control, by real actions or by thought process, the behavior of the people who are thought to be integral to the self. When a person is not able to separate, other people are felt to be maintaining the integrity of the self; they are held very closely to the self, near the self, or inside the self, and they are not allowed to be seen or treated as real, separate others.

We can hear this in counseling when a person comes in and says *My wife . . . My wife . . .*, or *My boyfriend . . . My boyfriend . . .*, or *The children . . . The children*. The topic is always *She . . . she . . . she . . .* and *He . . . he . . . he . . . .* The other person seems to loom larger than life. He or she is depersonalized and transformed, in fantasy, into only a nurturing breast, only a persecutor, only a dumping ground, only garbage or excrement, only a monster toward whom one needs to have no feelings, but only defenses.

It is not until a person is free-standing, able to let go of the ideal nurturing figure and the projected diabolical figure or monster figure, that the person can get anywhere near self-acceptance. Only a relatively well-integrated person can accept the self or anyone else. Holding onto these fantasy figures interferes with knowing the self and knowing the other. In order to know anyone, the person needs to achieve the position where he can say: *Whatever I am feeling, I am not conjoined with these other figures in such a way that I can't let go of them.* The person needs to learn, in gradual stages, that he can let go of someone without dying, disintegrating, or falling apart.

The more anxiety a person has, the more concrete the self seems to be, and the more dependent the person is on the concrete, constant evidence of relationship with another person. The other must be always present, or always on the telephone, or always giving gifts, or always in a good mood. The self is felt to exist only in the light of the parent's aproval, the friend's attention, the lover's passion, or the good opinion of others. It is as if the self exists, not in oneself as a whole being, but in fragments that are housed in other people. Other people, in turn, are seen only in this fantasy relation to the self—as nurturing and/or persecuting parents—and not in their own reality as others. And, when the self seems to exist only in another, losing that other—when the parent dies or the lover or child goes away—means *I will die.* Losing the other person seems to mean losing one's very self.

Separation anxiety often masquerades as love of a mate, filial duty to a parent, or devotion to a child. These are the more socially and personally acceptable masks for the terror of separation. We don't want to know this terror, this feeling of emptiness, panic, and dependence on others: first, because it is terrifying to know; then, because it is a childhood feeling and therefore seems shameful in an adult; and, perhaps most of all, because to know this clinging for what it is would mean having to begin to give it up, whereas one need not try to give up love, obedience, or devotion.

In fact, we can't really know our own terror of separation until we begin to separate. If this long, gradual, difficult task of childhood is only partially accomplished, it persists for the adult as an unresolved problem, a fearful and stressful effort. This is often the nameless problem that propels people into psychotherapy. Then the therapist may be able to help the person, through corrective experience, to continue the process of his own growth, and to build an integrated self that can stand alone.

INTEGRATION IN THERAPY

When this delayed, corrective integration takes place in therapy, it is the role of the therapist to show the person that inner and interpersonal spaces are safe—just as, for the child, it was a function of the parents to help him expand safe space in his inner and outer world. When the child whose parents were unable to show him a safe inner and outer world becomes an adult seeking help in psychotherapy, he has a "bad scene" to correct—the "primal scene" of his own childhood experience. In therapy, he is free to project this old scene of the secret theater, and in some ways to enact the dance or the play of the schizoid mechanism within the safe space of the therapeutic relationship.

This "acting out" also occurs in the person's other relationships, as we have discussed in the chapter on splitting and projection. But in the therapeutic relation, the results are different because, unlike the person's original family, his present family, or his friends and other associates, the therapist is (or becomes) aware of the script, and can view it from a position of helpful detachment. Whether the script or schizoid mechanism calls for an overprotective mother, a punitive, rejecting father, or for any other particular constellation of figures, the therapist is there to refuse to play the role, and yet to be aware of what the person is projecting, and to reflect back his projections through the lens of reality. The person speaks his familiar lines; but the therapist is there to respond, not with the parental or sibling voices that the patient is still unconsciously hearing, but with a voice that is kinder, more reliable, and more attentive to the real needs of the self. The therapist is there to make safe time through his reliable return and his devotion of the hour to the person's needs; and he is there to make, with his structuring and his silence, the safe space that was not available in childhood for the struggles of growth.

THE DEPRESSIVE RECOGNITION

Whenever and however integration of the self takes place, it involves an internalizing of good within the self: good figures, good experience, and good feelings. It also involves an internalizing of what is felt as *bad,* meaning that the person can contain in the self, and therefore can accept into his awareness, what is negative in the self and in others. For the child, this means that what is experienced as *bad*—confusion, rejection, reproach, negative or contradictory messages, fright, rage, anxiety, hateful fantasy, nightmares—does not become so predominant that it is overwhelming and can't be integrated into the self. For an adult going through the corrective integration of therapy, internalizing the bad involves what we call the *depressive recognition*.

The depressive recognition marks the end of manic flight and defense, and the end of splitting the self as a way of life. This doesn't mean, of course, that the person never runs from his problems or "splits" defensively when his feelings are too much to handle, or even that this recognition comes all at once. But the depressive recognition is an identifiable turning point, or series of turning points, in the effort to achieve a belated self-integration.

What we mean by the depressive recognition is that the person is able to take responsibility for the self as a separate person, and for his own "good" and "bad" thoughts, feelings, fantasies, and actions. Instead of projecting all the bad onto others, who are seen as powerful persecutors, depriving parents, and fearsome monsters; instead of seeking scapegoats for the failures of the self; instead of running frantically from depression; instead of splitting off his own feelings of fright and rage—the person begins to recognize and remember all aspects of his inner and outer world. This means that he recognizes weakness, mistakes, fears, and shortcomings. It means that he gives up denial and accepts confusion, loss, and sorrow.

There is no doubt that this recognition is painful and at times terrifying. That is why help is needed for the belated integration of an adult self, just as it is needed, from parents and other helpful figures, in order for a child to grapple successfully with the painful and terrifying aspects of his life. But the recognition of the bad that belongs to the self is as essential to life as a whole, separate, adult person as in the setting of limits on the bad that is alien to the self and taken in from others. The integrative process involves both taking in and shutting out, receptivity and expulsion, separating from others and joining with them. These processes are never complete, and their outcome is never perfect; but through them, we can hope to build, through growth and through corrective experience, what we might call a relatively integrated self.

The relatively integrated self can build upon itself and upon what is received from others. The integrated person can contain himself; good and bad feelings are manageable and can be held within this container. The good in the self isn't "pissed away" in chatter and flight and manic activity. The person's time and money are not wasted, but can be used for the purposes of the self. The person's expressions of affection are real, not ritualistic, because they are spoken from the whole self. The person's sexual impulses are not acted out compulsively or indiscriminately; they can be contained and integrated with tenderness and with aggression, in sexual play and sexual love, and in the context of relationships that have time to develop. The person's anger doesn't have to be dumped on the nearest available target, denied until it reaches explosive force, or dissipated even when its meaning is a signal for change: It can be held and directed where it belongs. The sad, depressed feelings of the integrated person reflect real sorrows; and these can be suffered and woven into the richness of the self.

FANTASY AND INTEGRATION

What and how must we integrate, in growing, to construct this kind of self? The love and care of the parents, and their own modeling of integration; our own bad feelings as well as our good feelings; what we are able to learn of reality; and our fantasies and those of our parents' fantasies that impinge on the self.

We must be very clear here about the sense in which we are using the word *fantasy*. On the deepest level, fantasy is biology; it has to do with what we do with our bodies. Fantasy is the mental reflection of all our actions. It is inhibited or rehearsed action. In this sense, fantasy accompanies everything we do—so we say that we *bite* into work, *grasp* mental concepts, are *stung* by insults, *re-member* ourselves.

But, as we have seen, the impinging of fantasy is different for the safe (or integrated) and the unsafe (or splitting) self. In psychotic states, fantasy combines with terror. In the nightmare, fantasy combines with terror. In the social nightmare, fantasy combines with terror. In creative work, however, fantasy recombines the elements of terror, domesticating the monster, making it into the laughing tiger of Selma Fraiberg's story in *The Magic Years* or the monstrously faulted hero of a Shakesperean tragedy: Art and play put the monster to work for the self. Creative fantasy works in a layer of the self between the fixed social code of acceptable thoughts and feelings and the fixed biological levels of our fears.

What does this mean in the separation/integration process? For the infant, all mental activity is a continuous stream related to action. the basis of fantasy in infancy is the sensorimotor system. Part of the development of mental life involves the coordination of sensorimotor systems and the separation of fantasy from action.

Fantasy, dreaming, and play are related activities which are organized by the basic needs of the individual at every stage of development. Whenever we are not scanning our environment or acting on it, we tend to return to basic internal scenarios. These scenarios are mainly concerned with getting food, maintaining body integrity, competing for attention, and expelling unpleasant experiences.

But fantasy doesn't mean simply images in the head. Because of its basis in the sensorimotor system, it arouses a complex set of responses involving muscular acts and hormonal secretions—the responses of what might be considered a sub-self. When we are in a fantasy, part of the self is divided from the present reality situation and taken into an encapsulated inner system which is irrelevant to the reality system and which is not affected by it.

Fantasy tends to repeat its own sequences, as in recurrent daydreams like those of Walter Mitty, or in dreams of being an important public figure or a movie star, or of meeting one's Prince or Princess Charming, or of writing the great American novel. These fantasies are recurrent "great expectations" of the future; or, sometimes, they are recurrent repetitions of past behavioral patterns—as when someone fantasizes beating up his childhood enemy or mentally addresses a dead or absent parent who is still very much present in the fantasy world.

Fantasy sequences can even structure institutions, such as the worlds of Hollywood movies and television, in which situation comedy, medical shows, detective series, Batman and its equivalents, and James Bond movies offer the social forms of repetitive fantasy. Again and again, death is averted; again and again, the hero triumphs; again and again, the cool, slick thinker wins, with the aid of his magical technology. Again and again, the family members perform their familiar set of moves to the sound of laughter meant to show the innocence of the game.

What does all this mean in the dynamics of separation and integration? Fantasies, dreams, and play are serious work—on some levels—for the child as for the adult. They do the work of bringing into the context of the self the elements of experience that are most difficult to contain: the monstrous feelings of fright and rage; the monstrous aspects of the parental figures; the incongruous, disharmonious, disproportionate, alarming, stressful, and bewildering aspects of our experience, as well as our seemingly more ordinary reality. This work goes on from the very beginning of childhood: The child discovers his senses and works on their messages, including those of the "sixth sense" or the "third ear," with every motion and with all the effort of his imagination. When fantasy, dreaming, and play are not able to work over the bodily and psychic experiences in such a way that they can be integrated into the self, these three activities take on their more distressing forms: anxious or psychotic fantasy, nightmares, and "acting out." Orientation to present reality is blocked by the split-off, projected scenarios.

When we say a child or adult is "acting out," we mean that a fantasy subsystem in the self—for example, the need for attention or to be "king of the hill"—errupts inappropriately into a person's real life space and interactions, impinging destructively on himself and on others, and perhaps destroying his relationships and his sphere of safety in the world. Acting out involves the dangerous process of confusing inner needs and social realities. Acting out is governed by the split self from the projection room of the secret theater. The need to act out the unintegrated needs left over from the past makes it unclear when and how it is safe to act or to express the real needs of the present. Acting out makes it unsafe to act at all, just as nightmares make it unsafe to dream, and just as fantasy which is infused with anxiety makes it unsafe to give oneself up to fantasy, and to its recreative and reconstructive functions.

It is important to distinguish between the constant stream of anxious worry or inner monologue and dialogue—which constitutes the mental imagery of a "normal neurotic" person—and the more developed mental process of imagination and creativity. When a person is anxious and cannot sleep, or when he is alone and can't sit still, he will have a constant bombardment of mental items; and he may even make a list of problems or worries in attempt to shed them. When such thinking can't be turned off and the mind won't let the body relax, this "thinking" is not functioning as a rehearsal for reality or problem-solving, which is one of the proper functions of fantasy. Instead, such "thinking" is a reaction formation against the fantasy of being empty, or perhaps worse, of being in contact with inner bad feelings. We have explored this pattern in the chapter on manic defenses. A rush of thoughts of this kind is a substitute for the feeling of security within the self. The inability to stop thinking is a clear sign of splitting and serious anxiety, a sign of the nonintegration of the self.

More useful to us than the flow of anxious thoughts or the recurrent fantasies involved with infantile fears is the process of constructing inner and outer realities or of modeling them for ourselves. This process of imagination enables us to appreciate and to be in touch with all the resources of experience we store inside ourselves, and to use this experience in fulfilling our individual and social needs.

On this third level, fantasy is part of the process of integration, rather than of the process of splitting. On an even higher level of integration, conscious thought may cease entirely; and then there is trust in the integrative process of the self. At this level, our dreams, plans, and wishes crystallize productively through their expression in the world of reality.

For the artist or the creative scientist, fantasy is simultaneously a defense against emptiness and destructive wishes and a social gift. Our culture, in the sense of our art, science, and social forms, is an integration of products of human imagination. These products in their cultural expression defend us against chaos, emptiness, and inner terrors while they canalize our efforts into constructive channels.

Art, dream, fantasy, and play are safe places for the working out of our destructive wishes, and for the catharsis of our rage, grief, and terror. We can dare to act in the world, and indeed to *be* in the world as separate selves, only as we are able to accomplish this working out: to harness our own forces, to integrate thought, feeling and experience, aggression and receptivity, into the context of a coherent self. When we can do so in the process of growing, or in the re-growing of the self in psychotherapy, we know that we can act without destroying ourselves or others, that we can feel without drowning in feeling, and that we can bear to live with others and inside ourselves.

Safe Space: The Rhythms of the Self

SEVEN

> *To everything there is a season, and a time to every purpose....*
> *Stop the world, I want to get off.*
> *I am alone with the beating of my heart.*

Human life is rhythmic from beginning to end. From the rhythms of ovulation and copulation that begin it, through the long, slow rhythms of the life cycle which finally bring it to an end, our life is ebb and flow, hunger and satiation, waking and sleep. The self, our organism, is a rhythmic oscillator, responsive to our own bodily and emotional processes and to the cyclic motions of the physical world.

We are all aware, to some extent, of these rhythms and cycles, and also of their elaboration in our particular culture. Day and night, the seasons of the year, the phases of the moon and the menstrual cycle of women, the school year, the fiscal year, the work week and the weekend, meals and paychecks—all these familiar measures comprise the clock that marks our personal and cultural time.

A major problem for a person in making safe space and time is to be in touch with the rhythms of the self, of others, and of the society in wuch a way that he feels secure—just as the infant learns its safety in the basic familiar rhythms of rocking, feeding, and sleep. Troubled people usually feel out of touch, out of tune, and out of harmony with themselves and with the social rhythms. When we are troubled we feel time moving either too fast or too slowly; we rush through time or feel frozen in it; and we suffer a sense of interference with our own timing and a disturbance of our own natural patterns. In such disturbed time, when we are not trapped by others, we paralyze ourselves; when we are not pressured by others, we rush ourselves and interrupt ourselves.

RHYTHMIC NEEDS

To know the self, to be in touch and in tune with the self, is to know the rhythms of the self in the most fundamental way—to know the needs of the self. Some of these needs are very primitive: to sleep, to eat, to excrete, to have stimulation and relaxation. These seem like very basic, simple, self-evident processes. Yet troubled people forget and frustrate these needs. They forget to sleep; and they forget to eat when they are hungry—or perhaps they overeat, unaware that they are satiated. They forget to relax, and continue to rush along at a manic tempo; or they forget to seek stimulation, and remain sunk in depressed, dead time.

How can a person be so out of touch with the needs of the self when we know that the body has its own wisdom? People originally lose the sense of their own basic needs in deference to the needs of people they grow up with, and sometimes to the needs of the culture. The rhythm that a child is in touch with is not so much the rhythm of the self as it is the rhythm of the mother and father. If that rhythm is depressed, obsessional, or hysterical, the child internalizes that rhythm. In fact, the child will internalize the rhythm of anyone who is important to his life.

Consequently, it may be difficult, later, to ask oneself *How do I feel?* and to get a clear or truthful answer, even from one's own body. The child, and later the adult, who goes into the self and asks *How do I feel?* contacts, rather than *I'm tired* or *I'm hungry,* some portion of the parental rhythm, or a reaction in the self against the parental rhythm. The growing person may learn to behave like the parents, or to behave in an opposite way in order to avoid the rhythm of the parents. If a parent has low energy and is hypochondriacal or oversolicitous about the child, the child may learn to feel *Maybe I'm sick* more readily than the average person; or he may learn to ignore the bodily signals of sickness or need for rest through refusal to become like the parent or to accept the parental interference. If a parent is very depressed, the child may either take on the depression or seek to compensate for it by being super-manic—always lively, always cheerful, always trying to avoid the dead rhythm of the parent.

Many people are very much afraid to be alone, fearing that aloneness means that they will go blank, with nothing happening inside the self. This is what happens to a person who is very suppressed, depressed, oppressed, or repressed: The natural rhythms of the self are pushed down under great pressure and can't come to the surface. The rhythms of the self can't be expressed. When such a person begins, through psychotherapy or some other means of growth, to bring the self out into the open, he or she may begin to play the piano, to dance, or to swim—to engage in some active form of expression of a rhythmic feeling. The person's physical, sexual, and emotional rhythms begin to seek their expression in daily life.

Getting in touch with the self is largely getting in touch with these rhythms in the self: the sexual needs, the other bodily needs, the needs for stimulation and for rest. The person begins to do things that express the felt inner needs of the self, instead of only pleasing the parents, pleasing the mate, pleasing the children, or pleasing the world of others with their expectations and demands. The person who is in touch with the self is also, of course, in touch with the rhythms of others. Any close relationship demands our response to the rhythmic needs of the other person, and to love someone is, partially, to take on the rhythms of the other. But that is different from being driven by the alien, insistent rhythms of another person, in ignorance or ignoring of the needs of the self.

CONFLICTING RHYTHMS

When a person finds the self dancing to the tune of another drummer or another piper, or to the rhythms of an earlier time of life, the first task is to become sensitive to his own signals of resentment and alienation. Many people feel resentful and don't know why. Many people are always engaged in either acting out or fighting off the rhythms of another person and another time. The oscillations of the self are being driven and speeded up, or damped down and suppressed by the outside driver. This outside force may even be a machine, as when a person works on an assembly line; or it may be the process of commuting to work, the hectic pace of a particular occupation or the slowed time of a retired or unemployed person, or the frenzied, yet empty time of many housewives.

Many people feel trapped in the externally imposed rhythms of their own daily lives—or even of their own mates. We all know couples who are perpetually out of phase with each other: one always dragging his feet, the other always straining ahead like a restless racehorse. Sometimes a couple will show such a tragicomic mismatching of rhythms in a very graphic form every time they walk down the street: One is always a step or two ahead, the other dragging along behind, each resenting the natural rhythm of the other.

Violation of a person's own natural rhythms is a profound violation of the self. There is always violence and splitting in the self when this occurs. The child may go alone with the insistent rhythm of a parent who is always saying, *Hurry up! What makes you so slow?* But the actions are performed under the duress of anxiety, tension, and resentment: The parental voice may be internalized, so that the person is always saying to himself, *Hurry up! You're too slow!* But at the same time, in secret, another voice is saying, *No, I won't; You can't make me.*

The child in this kind of conflict may become a person who moves at the quicker pace, but who always makes mistakes, always stumbles over his own feet. Or he may do things so carelessly that they have to be redone, or he may never quite finish what he starts. He appears to be carrying out the parent's wishes and his own conscious intentions, but in the reality of the inner self those wishes are persistently defied and sabotaged. On the other hand, the child who is always pressured and rushed may balk and move even more slowly, frustrating even his own rhythm of activity in order to fend off the imposed rhythm of the parents.

Another child may be expected to slow her own natural pace, to be less active because she exhausts the parents, to be less quick to learn because intelligence pressures her peers and siblings and threatens teachers unaccustomed to its demands. Intelligence can be a social handicap. Adults sometimes say of a child: *He's ahead of himself,* which could have the meaning, *Some of his capacities are more developed than others,* but which more often means, *He's ahead of what we think he should be doing.* The child who is "behind" or "ahead" is really "slow" or "fast" only in terms of the timeclock of expectations imposed on him by other people and by the culture; or perhaps he is reacting against these extrinsic rhythms.

The social timeclock itself is partly the product of experience with many children, presented exhaustively by experts for the guidance of parents; and it is partly an expression of the rate and kind of development necessary to produce, in turn, adults who can move to the rhythms of our culture. Culture itself must observe rhythms that can be tolerated by human beings in a given environment—so that it is easy to understand why life in tropical regions proceeds more slowly. But human nature is so malleable, and human beings so ingenious in their adaptations, that there is enormous range in the rhythms of activity in various cultures, and in various families and milieux within a culture. The rhythms of New York City are very different from the rhythms of small Midwestern towns, and of isolated ranches on the Great Plains. These examples themselves suggest that time has something to do with space, that constricted and overpopulated space contracts social time, and that multiplication of social molecules speeds up their action.

The relationship between social space and experienced time certainly is not that simple; but it is so intimate that we even use space as a metaphor for time: We speak of "the space of an hour" or "the span of a month," or of concerns that take up "too much space" in our lives. We say, "There's a time and place for everything." We experience space and time together, measured by our inner map and our inner clock. We can think of space, the arrangement of objects in space, and of colors and forms in an art object, as a kind of visual and bodily rhythm. We can think of time spatially, as a desert stretching before us, as a blank page on a calendar; or we think of a span of time as a "breathing space" between ourselves and the demands of others, a "safe space" for the self. We can experience the disorder of objects in space much as we experience the confusion of events in time. People who value neatness are often fond of schedules; the ordering of both space and time enhances their feeling of security. People who are "loose" with space are often "loose" with time; they may require less definition, less predictability, less structuring. We can feel interruptions of our private time much as we feel invasions of our private space. "Safe space" for the self often means a place, such as home or a study room, where one's time is safe from interruption; while "safe time" often means the time spent in a special place or with a special person.

We hold other people at a distance, or accept them into closeness, largely on the basis of whether they disturb or enhance our own rhythms, whether their timing is congruent with our own. We have spoken already of the ebb and flow of need and fulfillment between the infant and the mothering person. From infancy, through childhood and into our adult lives, we are able to be truly responsive to the timing of others to the degree that our own rhythms have been respected. To the extent that we have been allowed our own time—to feed, to sleep, to develop our human capacities—to that extent we can allow others their time and their sense of timing. To the extent that we are forced, pressured, and interrupted in our own processes of others or to try to bring the whole self into a mutual rhythm with another person. Instead we must force, pressure, interrupt, and frustrate our parents, our mates, our children, our friends, and our selves.

We see, then, people in adult life who cannot allow, to themselves or others, safe time or inviolate inner space. Safe space really means room to be oneself, not cut off from others but in relationships which allow separateness. Safe time really means that the self can be rested and fed, and that its capacities for giving and effort can be renewed. In safe time and safe space we regroup our forces, we reintegrate ourselves again and again. The life of every day abrades the self, and its threats and anxieties penetrate our inner space with anxious fantasy and nightmare. In leisure, privacy, and silence, alone or with people who ease us with their own responsive rhythms, we may have our repair. But that repair can occur only if we experience enough, in the earlier stages of life or in a corrective process of therapy, of what safe time *is* and what safe space *is,* of what it is to have time to enter our own inner space, and what it is to have a relationship of safe space that is developed over time, so that we do not repetitively destroy our own time and spoil our own space.

We are dealing, at any given time, with our own bodily rhythms, including our own developmental and aging process. We also deal with the rhythms and moods of people close to us; with the cultural and societal rhythms; with the temporal rhythms of night and day, season and climate; and with the rhythms of interaction—of separating and joining, of coming close together and moving apart, of giving and receiving, ups and downs. We can understand the complexity of these processes in very concrete terms if we imagine a day in the life of any family, whose members not only have their own personalities but who are at various stages of the life cycle, each with its own intrinsic and extrinsic necessities. For the mother at home with young children, the day may have a long, slow curve; yet the line of the curve is jagged with interruption: The time may seem empty, yet offer no breathing space; and even the night may be penetrated with the needs of an infant or child, so that the mother's rhythm of activity and rest must be adapted to the shorter time spans of the child. In this stage of the family life cycle, the rhythmic process of the parents is disrupted; and sexuality, conflict, sharing, and repose may become more difficult and complex because they cannot always take place or be completed at the time they are desired. Sometimes parents with young children, or older parents with adolescents, neglect the need to make room for their own privacy and their own interactions; like infants discouraged with the feeding process, they may become accustomed to never having their needs satisfied, and their relationship may suffer simply from lack of inviolate time together. More hopefully, parents, like children, can be adaptive enough in their rhythms to satisfy their needs to eat, sleep, talk together, argue, play, and have sex at times compatible with the rhythms of their family lives.

There are still other rhythms that must be integrated. For adults who go out to work, and for children who go to school, the day and the week have a particular shape which includes the pressure of early morning and "getting everybody out"; the bustle and hunger of dinner time impinging on the fatigue and the need to unwind at the end of the day; the conflicting needs, on the weekend, to rest, to play, and yet to accomplish the work of the household. If only one parent works, that parent's need for repose at home may intersect with the other's need to be more active and to "get out of the house." If both are working, they may need to plan adaptations that are humane in terms of their mutual need for rest, yet receptive to the rhythmic needs of their children for food and attention.

The rhythms of adolescents often depart sharply from the family patterns. In their drive to separate and to begin to make a life on their own, adolescents and even young adults very often go "far out" in exploring their own rhythms and rebelling against what adults regard as "given" in life. They may deny the need to sleep or to eat according to the social or familial clock; and they may, like infants, "get their days and nights turned around," eat their own menu on their own idiosyncratic schedules, and in general try to "march to a different drummer." However exasperating to parents, this tendency is part of the process of exploring the maturing self and its capacities and demands; and only with time and maturation are these "rhythms of the self" brought again into some degree of accord with social requirements.

We are saying, then, that both in growing and in our lives as adults we experience our own personal rhythms of space and time, sometimes harmoniously blended and sometimes in conflict with the rhythms of others and their expectations. We are not talking, of course, only about the rhythms of every day. To "rush" a child doesn't mean only to hurry him in tying his shoes. It may also mean the arbitrary speeding or slowing of his developmental clock, as when a parent puts the young child on the toilet at an age before his own rhythms can possibly lead him there, or treats an adolescent as if he is still a young child. This problem is made more complex by the fact that children and other people often try to rush their own inner timepiece or freeze its hands. Again, the wish to slow or to hurry time magically doesn't refer only to the passing minutes and hours of a day, although we are all familiar with how time seems to drag or to rush past us, depending on what we are doing. People also wish to play tricks with the life cycle. The adolescent is not only often misperceived by her parents, but she often misperceives herself, trying to rush into adulthood, and yet trying, at other times, to prolong childhood. And we all know people who try to cling to youth or to recapture its hope and romance. Others drive themselves grimly into achievements as if there is "no time to waste" or to ripen; and still others behave as if time were not passing: Only as they enter middle age do they begin to realize that it *has* passed without their yet choosing what to do with their lives.

THE LIFE CYCLE

Of all our bodily rhythms, the life cycle is on the largest scale and has the longest measures. Like all our bodily rhythms, it is inexorable; although, as with our other rhythms, we can try to speed it, to slow it, to force it, to interrupt it, to freeze its motion, to deny its signals.

For the child, the major vehicle of growth is play. The child's play orders his world and gives expression to the growing self. A child is small, frail, immature, dependent on others and subject to their wills. But in play, the child is master or mistress, creating the world of play and controlling all its happenings. In play, the child has a chance to explore the world in a manageable form. In imagination, he lives his way into the roles of the adult as well as the fantasy roles created by his wishes, hopes and fears.

"Child's play", then, is very serious. It is the child's way of integrating experience and feeling, fantasy and reality. We have shown, in previous chapters, some of the rhythmic needs and processes involved in growth, and the to-and-fro process of separation and integration of the self. The child's play is a vehicle for that process. It is the child's way of exploring his world and, through the use of fantasy, becoming intimate with reality.

The play world has its own limits, defined by the child and also incorporated from the outside world with its rules, roles, and games. Children at play together understand these limits and the freedom that lies within them. The limits of play, and the fact that it is "pretending" and not "real" make it a safe space for self-expression, for the exploration of feeling and for the development of a viable self.

Play explores possibility, it explores the realm of the future, as well as that of one's wildest dreams. Play enables the child to separate from familiar patterns and to explore new ways to be. Play offers the child the chance to live, in fantasy and in feeling, in many worlds, each related to the real world of the self by a deep, unconscious bond. In play, the child can domesticate the monsters of fantasy, bringing them under his own control. When play is employed as the arena for taming the child's monsters, they are put in their place, and the fears and desires they represent trespass less upon his action and perception in reality. Thus play is a major means of integration, as well as a major indicator of a child's fears, wishes and concerns. Many disturbed children cannot play, fearing to release their powerful feelings and fantasies into the realm of action. Psychotherapists who work with such children help them to experience play as a safe life space in which to express their feelings and to work out their problems.

As we grow, our play becomes ever more realistic, just as our action in the real world becomes more effective. We can see development as a process of learning how to fulfill the needs of the self in reality, and how to make a viable reality out of our fantasies. This is, in a sense, the mirror image of what we call "acting out". Play and dreams remain, even beyond childhood, safe spaces for acting out what we wish for and what we fear, and our shared fantasies are also elaborated into fiction, drama, and other art forms. As long as we can make spontaneous use of these safe life spaces, in response to the rhythms of our emotional needs, our tendency to distort what we see and feel remains within bounds.

For the pre-adolescent and the adolescent, exploration of the world takes place increasingly in a more ritualized form of play, that of sports and other games. More private fantasies are pursued in daydreams and in responses to television, films, and popular music. The adolescent is engaged, as we have seen, in accomplishing separation as an adult self. He is also engaged in testing his own capacities and his own unique personality in whatever arenas he can find or make for himself.

If, for the child, access to play as a means of exploration and integration is crucial to growth, a vital aspect of adolescent development is finding one's own voice, and learning to use it in such a way that the self is recognized. This must happen in the family, in the peer group, and in the larger networks of school, work and community as the growing person becomes a young adult. The adolescent, with a changing body and a changing voice, confronts a bewildering world even when he looks inward. In exploring the outside world, much of his task is to learn to discriminate between practicable plans and wishful thinking—between what he dreams of doing, what he wishes he could do, what he intends to do, and what he actually does.

These are distinctions which are much more likely to present problems for the adolescent than for the younger child, who has more latitude for play and less scope for action in the larger world. The adolescent, in leaving the family and growing into adulthood, is really entering new territory; he has to make new maps of his environment and new clocks for measuring his own progress toward his goals. He has to learn the capacity to live with and regulate his own rhythms, and to synchronize them with social time. He must achieve, by the time he is an adult, some recognition of the real, though not wholly fixed, limits of his scope and his powers.

We are not uncomfortable with an adult identity until self-image and social recognition coincide. For the adolescent, this means he must not only learn to use his voice but must learn to match his words with deeds, so that what he says and what he does can make him a socially recognized life space in which to emerge and grow. This "voicing", and the independent action that validates it, become in adolescence a vital means of separation from the parents and achievement of an adult self.

This task of development involves struggle, competition, and striving with others. It also involves, for the adolescent, as for the person at any other stage of separation and individuation, some struggling with his own intense ambivalence about becoming himself and depending on himself. We can see this ambivalence in the way the adolescent treats the rhythms of his own personal development. Sometimes he tries to hurry time, rushing into adulthood in fantasy while overlooking what he must do in order to become truly adult. At other times, he clings to childhood, trying to stop the hands of the clock or turn them back, seeking the comforts of lost dependency.

This kind of struggle with time is not unique to adolescence, although we see it in rather extreme forms at this period of development. We all suffer, in one way or another, in one life space or another, from the desire to slow time or to speed it, to pass quickly over one portion of our lifetime and linger in another. The adolescent desire to be some other age than one presently is becomes, later in life, the desire to be ageless, the wish to deny aging, time, and death. For time requires a continual giving up of previous pleasures, patterns and attachments. Our anxiety about time and its changes is in part a profound form of separation anxiety. For the adolescent growing into adulthood, the fruits of independence are not free; they have a cost. This cost is the giving up of the security and pleasure of being fed by others.

The adolescent, in becoming a separate person, leaves a relatively safe life space, in which he is fed and cared for, for a new territory that becomes safe only as his own exploration makes it so. This exploration of a new life space is the essential preoccupation of the young adult. It may involve activity that is very wide in its range and hectic in its pace. This exploration is necessary as a prelude to the selection of a life, the clearing of one's own life space in the form of choosing an important person with whom to share one's life and committing oneself to a work role. This was easier in the past, when the culture defined our roles more clearly, and we lived where our parents lived and did what our parents did. The task is harder now, because in many ways we must make our own maps and discover our own rhythms.

THE MID-LIFE CRISIS

Because the rhythmic curve of the life cycle is so long, it is only as we move into mid-life that we begin to see it as a whole and to ask seriously the question: *Where have I come from? Where am I going?* Someone said that "no young man believes he will ever die." But the person in mid-life begins to know that he or she *is* going to die.

In mid-life, a person experiences a crisis of the acceptance of time and death. We become lost, like Dante, in a dark forest of fears and confusion. If worked through appropriately, with a depressive recognition and determined facing of our life situation, we experience a productive reversal, accompanied by a liberation of energy and creativity. We find the path. If not, we deteriorate.

What is this life-giving reversal? At the onset of the mid-life crisis, a man or a woman is compelled to perceive signs of aging. It might happen because a parent dies. Sometimes it occurs through recognition of the maturation of an adolescent child. The recognition of change in one's life position is not direct—*I am older*—but indirect: *If my parent dies, I am next. If my son (daughter) is dating already, I must be older.* When the role of parent or child must be relinquished, there is an emptiness. Sometimes at the onset of the crisis, a person feels let down at work, either because success does not bring an anticipated fulfillment, or because lack of success brings increasing frustration. The person in mid-life crisis asks, *Is this all there is?* He or she has feelings of lost or wasted time and of missing "really living," accompanied by a terror of dying. People often take flight at this point: into affairs with young people, as a denial of aging; into alcohol; into delusional projects—flying saucers, seances, life after death, miracle cures, etc. A person may also try to accelerate his life pace—making many new beginnings, but finishing nothing.

All forms of flight express rejection of the self, refusal to accept the current life situation, rage at one's immediate family, and fear of experience. Part of the self is held back out of the stream of time, seeking to swim upriver like a salmon toward adolescence. The feeling is, *I don't want now, not this life, this body—can't I do it over?* Like Don Juan and the Sleeping Beauty, the person keeps searching for a lost ideal.

Flight is often flight from guilt. *My mother died—and I did not do enough to keep her alive.* This feeling is intolerable; and one flees from it. So is the feeling of having betrayed one's own creativity, or the feeling of damaging a son or daughter. Unless we have help, we cannot work through the depression caused by such feelings, and we will sink under them or run away.

DENYING DEATH AND TIME

The denial of death is the unreal conflict that needs to be overcome in the mid-life crisis. The denial of dying is an "unreal" conflict because what is feared is *not dying as an experience*—but an *image* of death based on the child's panic of emptiness, loss, disintegration, and mutilation. This confusion of image and experience can literally scare the breath out of a person. A person scared to death by images forgets to breathe; and he does not live life so much as he lives defenses against a fantasy of dying. Such frightened people find it impossible to be alone or to give good gifts to themselves. They are always running—from the past, the future, and the present.

Flight often takes the disguised form of a symbiotic marriage. The husband and wife will feel glued together, raging at each other but clinging to each other, each stuck to an infantile position in the false "marriage." Each is saying: *I am a child and you must be the good mother/father I never had.* Time is negated in this process, as is responsibility for recognizing the shift in the balance of interpersonal power that occurs as a person matures. Consequently, such a death-denying person is always living to get something *from* someone, or to pay back someone for not giving, or to "show" (i.e. spite) someone. There is no feeling that life is *for me,* no feeling of doing things for the self. When time and death are denied, the full experimental space of adult powers is given over to the child's rage. The child's fear of being separate—of being paralyzed, of being empty, of being attacked, of not getting nurture and recognition, of dying—devours the adult personality, inch by inch. The denial of dying enthrones death inside the personality. Only by accepting ourselves and by living in our own rhythm can we feel secure that we are giving no ground to death, to rage, to fright, to resentment.

The reversal in attitude described here sees a person moving from an envious, deprived, and bitter position—*is this all there is?*—to a receptive and grateful one—*I have all this richness of life in and around me.* Such enjoyment becomes the basis of a mature capacity to give gifts, to be creative. Passage through the rapids of the mid-life crisis is marked by the welling up of self-trust, and of a rhythmic sense that experience can be enjoyed.

Our flight can be turned into facing ourselves, suffering, learning, reducing guilt from death wishes, clarifying bad feelings, mourning, and, eventually, opening good experience. If we can let go of the need to re-live the past, we can involve ourselves with the present. There is time to live, even though we are dying. *Because* we know we are dying, time takes on new value. We cannot afford to use our precious gift of time in running, blaming, and bickering. We are responsible for every moment of our experience. We accept the bad (with limits) as the condition of being alive. Our old nemesis and persecutor, death, becomes a friend, an ally against the real enemy of our life—the deathly fear of being alive that freezes our capacity to experience. When our anxiety is stilled, we can see "infinity in a grain of sand and eternity in an hour."

The recognition of death is the most profound of our "depressive recognitions." We face our death like a child facing bedtime. First, we cling to the illusion that we can ignore it. Then, as it intrudes, we fight against it, dreading the end of light and of consciousness, fearing to sleep, and—yes—"perchance to dream," fearing the nightmare waiting for us in the void. Yet even children finally welcome sleep, for no one can enjoy an endless day; and similarly we see aged people reluctantly accept their waning powers, their need for rest, their need, finally, to put an end to life. Even if, in Dylan Thomas' words, we "Do not go gentle into that good night" but "Rage, rage against the dying of the light," the rhythms of light and darkness, waking and sleeping, birth and dying are deep in our being as they were in infancy. We grow weary, and our enemy becomes our friend; like sleep, death is our friend. The fear of death robs us of sleep, but the acceptance of death gives us the appreciation of time. Socrates said that philosophy—meaning knowing how to live—is the art of dying.

The major problem with facing death and dying is the confusion of dying with an image of death constructed by the child in us out of our terror of separation, disintegration, emptiness, and encapsulation. These forms of terror, whether they involve nightmares of being buried alive, dismembered, or being mutilated, or bleeding to death, derive their power from childhood anxiety. Our worst fears of death and dying derive, not from the actual process of death and dying, but from our own projections.

The denial of death is often considered to be, not only the basis of mental disorders, but also the basis of personality structure, and even the basis of cultural forms. The denial of death takes several forms as various beliefs in immortality. For example, people believe in the physical or psychic afterlife as a continuation of the ego. People also hold tenaciously to the belief that genetic continuity will confer a form of immortality; and consequently they strive to control their children's lives as a way of extending their own personality. A third form of immortality is the use of one's creative work to reinforce a fantasy of rebirth in other people through one's work. Another form of belief in immortality is pantheistic, and relies upon the immortality of soul stuff in its identity with natural processes. This form of immortality is presented strongly through romantic poetry and some forms of mysticism.

It is arguable, of course, that we are one with nature, that our genes do persist, that our works do persist, and that even our most elevated psychic states may be transmitted to or through others. But our main concern here is with how our image of death or immortality may deform our actual experience of living in such a way that fear of dying becomes a way of life.

One of our major strategies for avoiding death is the refusal to be born into any state of aliveness. Children often make a deal with themselves, saying in essence, *If I don't risk coming alive in my feelings, they can't be mutilated.* Adults often maintain this bad bargain with life, feeling *If I don't love anyone, I can't be hurt; If I don't give myself fully in a sexual experience, I can't lose myself; If I don't commit myself to anything or anyone, I can't suffer loss or disappointment; If I don't really live, I will never have to face death.*

All involvement in experience involves risk, and all fright can be understood ultimately as the fear of dying. This fear is seldom conscious, but we can learn to recognize it in tension, in anxiety, and in the withholding of the self from any deep penetration. In the fear of being destroyed and of destroying others, a person is afraid to penetrate another or to be penetrated, to go inside someone or to allow someone into one's body or one's self.

YIELDING TO SEXUAL RHYTHMS

When people are afraid of the sexual process, they are often afraid that they are going to be damaged or that they will damage the other person; as in an outburst of aggression, they are afraid of killing or being killed. Like our other fantasies, this may sound extreme, even bizarre; but not so much so when we remember the sources of fantasy in our earliest perceptions and in our biological heritage as animals with hands, teeth, rage, and the power to kill.

Much of this fear is based, as we have discussed earlier, on the "primal scene," the child's experience of the relationship of mother and father. If the child was aware of rage in the parents and felt that the mother and father fought and mutilated each other, then the adult's notion of interaction and interpenetration between a man and a woman is contaminated by a powerful and persistent fantasy of destruction. A woman may feel that it is unsafe to let a man enter her body. A man may be unable to experience a woman's body as a safe place to enter. A woman, as a result of her fear, may be frigid or inhibited in her sexual responses and in her own sexual aggressiveness. A man may suffer some degree of impotence, or premature ejaculation, or difficulty in reaching a climax. A person may feel, on a deep, unconscious level of the self, that to engage in intercourse in a fully involved way would mean being mutilated, bitten, swallowed or spat out, and, finally, emptied into a void.

These underlying fears have tremendous power; and we can measure that power by the defenses, the avoidances, the efforts to place limits on involvement, and the controls a person sets up in this most intimate and most rhythmic of our interactions. A person may perform sexual acts, yet he may always keep his distance; a person may submit sexually, yet not respond. A person may participate physically in the act, yet he may not allow the emotions to be engaged. A man may complain, *She goes along with it, but she never acts as if she really wants me.* A woman may say, *He always closes his eyes, he never says my name, he never says he loves me; its like I'm not there or he's not there.*

People may develop habits of fatigue, minor ailments, nursed resentments, or concocted arguments in order to avoid their sexual life. Couples may always quarrel after having sex, sometimes because of the lack of involvement and therefore of full satisfaction; sometimes to cancel out pleasure, for which they feel guilty and fear punishment; or sometimes to parry the threat of increased closeness to the other person. People have many ways of diluting, avoiding, interrupting, damaging, undoing, and destroying experience which threatens to become too intense—so intense that one may "lose oneself" in it.

Full sexual involvement is like going down in an elevator into the deepest levels of the self. It means some letting go of the conscious self, of the control of the watchful ego, and giving oneself up to the deepest bodily rhythms of the self and of the other person.

This letting go may bring into play the deepest fears we have, as it also expresses our deepest needs. When the ego's control is relaxed in the rhythmic return to sexual experience, we have the recurrent chance to be most fully in our bodies, and to reclaim the energies of the primitive self. In sexual love and sexual play in their most spontaneous and most developed forms, what is primitive in us is integrated with what is civilized; our aggression is integrated with our tenderness.

This presupposes a self that can dare to let go of its usual level of inhibition, a self that is not full of dammed-up rage; it presupposes that the person does not in fact have to fear destructiveness in the self or in the other. Full involvement in the sexual act means being able to trust the self and to trust the other. The full release and full reception of sexual energies requires accepting the self and the other, accepting one's own real body and the real body of the other person, and accepting the power of the bodily rhythms.

To achieve this level of trust, acceptance, integration, and spontaneity is very difficult. Becoming socialized, after all, has involved much training in inhibition, much restraint by the ego of the primitive forces of the self. And we live in a culture that serves the addictive appetites of the body better than it serves the fundamental needs of the bodily self. We are accustomed to the

Safe Space: The Rhythms of the Self

phenomena of food without nourishment, sleep without rest, work without commitment, activity without purpose, contact without involvement, sex without love, and life without the acceptance of aging and of death. We know how to feed babies away from the breast, how to milk cows by machine, how to feed people at a great distance from the land where the food is grown and the animals killed. We know how to relegate childbirth and illness to hospitals, psychosis and aging to institutions, and death to funeral parlors festooned with euphemisms. We have a great deal of practice in evading and cushioning our awareness of the processes of nature and of our own bodies. We say this not to romanticize pain or the struggles of life in a simpler culture, but rather to note how easy it is, in our culture, to be estranged from our bodily needs and rhythms, and from full awareness of the rhythms of nature.

Even without this cultural estrangement, and even without the leftover fright of the primal scene of early experience, there is an element of awe and terror in full bodily and emotional experience. Women who have given birth in full consciousness know the overwhelming rhythmic force of the body when the time comes to push the baby out, and the terrifying fantasies about what is happening to the body that may accompany that unprecedented moment. Perhaps, just as a person falling asleep may startle awake with a feeling of falling through space, we may also know an instant of natural terror in letting go of our rational controls and yielding to the full power of the sexual urge, or of grief, or of love. In such moments of irresistible emotion, we sense ourselves as a leaf in the wind, or as a swimmer afloat in the strong current of a river.

Our task, then, is to go with the tide, yet not to drown; to yield to our own internal currents, yet also to channel and contain them. The integrated adult self can perform this constant task, not at all times and not in all life spaces at any given time, but with a consistent and often renewed awareness of self and of one's receptivity to others. To develop such a self is what we strive for, in growing and in the corrective regrowing of psychotherapy. The best evidence of integration is our capacity to relax, to be in our own time and in our own life space. When we are able to integrate and to humanize our own forces, then there is no need to deny and deform our own rhythmic needs. Then we are able to move and to rest—to live, not in splitting or in flight, but in safe space and time. Then we are able to express in freedom and to receive in relaxation the rhythms of work, love, rest, play, and sleep.

Waking from the Social Nightmare

EIGHT

> *If I am not for myself, who is for me?*
> *If I am for myself alone, what am I?*
> *If not now, when?*
> *When will the world be mine?*

Once we know and live in our own rhythms, we still must live with the rhythms of the culture. Once we wake from our own private nightmares and take possession of their meanings, we find ourselves still living in the social nightmare, among the monsters projected by our society in its efforts to deal with history, with terror, with the integration of different people, and with the collective needs and frustrations of its members.

SOCIAL INTEGRATION

The parallel between individual and society cannot be made simplistically exact. Yet there is a close parallel to be made between the integrative tasks of the individual self, with which we have been concerned through most of this book, and the integrative tasks of a society. Like an individual, every society has to find ways of dealing with its own conflicts and its own needs. Like an individual, every society has the problem of channeling its own aggressive forces into forms that can contain them, and, as much as possible, into forms in which they can be utilized as energies for the good of the whole.

We have discussed this problem as it relates to the individual self, and we have also considered the signs and expressions of unfinished integration in an individual. The split self, the self in manic flight, the self stuck in symbiotic forms of relationship, the self locked onto the track of the schizoid mechanism: All these express failed or incomplete processes of integration. For the poorly integrated self, the monsters wait beneath the surface of unconsciousness, and the wholeness of the self is constantly threatened from within by the needs that remain unmet and by the violence that remains unintegrated and uncontained.

Society, at once a collection and a synthesis of individual needs and strivings, relates to this problem in two ways. On the one hand, the society collectively expresses the levels of integration of its members and their group forms. On the other, the society as a whole reinforces or frustrates the individual self in its integrative struggles. Through the social forms of empathic response or schizoid non-response and coercion, the society reduces or confirms the splitting and flight of the individual self. Like the family, the society encourages its members to be persons, or restricts them as objects.

RELATIONSHIPS AS SAFE SOCIAL SPACE

To grow in an integrated way, a person requires good *pair* relationships, an empathic social *group,* and a social *network* that offers recognition of his gifts and of his needs. These elements are basic to the expansion of safe social space. We have discussed the role, in growing, of the original pair relationship with the mothering person. As adults, we still need to "pair" with another, whether on a lifelong basis or in more transient and partial relationships.

But as we grow, the pair relationship is no longer enough; we also know ourselves increasingly as members of social groups. We leave our first group—the family—and go outside to play; we go to school and find friends, and, as we come into adolescence, we look ever more seriously to our peers as models and as interpreters and reflectors of ourselves. As we become adults, we know ourselves to be members of larger and larger groups: a neighborhood, a locality, a society, a culture, the human race.

There is no saving *idea* that makes safe space for a human being. What works for an individual is always *relationship*, never isolated experience or function. We have to ask, then, as we look for safe social space, how we may fare in relating ourselves to a society that has its own patterns of splitting and of flight; and how, even if we grow or regrow as relatively integrated selves, we can invest ourselves in meaningful ways in a social context that denies meaning.

A major problem for all of is the interface between personal and social problems. For therapists, the problem is dual. The client or patient asks, *What do you mean, I don't need to be mistrustful? Look at the corrupt government, the dog-eat-dog economy, crime in the streets. It's every man for himself in this world; nobody else gives a damn.* How can we oppose these social attitudes with an ideal of empathy? And how can we satisfy our political commitment—our commitment to the social body—without sacrificing empathic behavior?

Our main tool is discrimination. Everyone knows that, in a society which is far from utopian, all our ideals for human interaction need to be modified—as, indeed, all ideals suffer modification in reality. In a highly competitive society, the self must be guarded; and trust, openness, and authenticity may be carried only so far. The transparent, vulnerable self is too naked for this world.

But modifying our ideals, and being selective in their application, does not mean that we must sacrifice our goals. It means, rather, that we must be constantly alert to the distinctions between our societal reality and our own fantasy; between outer events and our own inner responses; between the present, real situation and our remembrance and reconstruction of the past; between the social nightmare and our own personal monsters. A person may experience scapegoating in the family, in school, and at work—but this does not mean that safe space cannot be constructed except through withdrawal.

THE INTEGRATIVE TASK OF PSYCHOTHERAPY

These discriminations are so difficult to make, for some people most of the time and for most people some of the time, that psychotherapists and other "helpers" in our society take on a dual role. On the one hand, they offer safe space and time to the individual who struggles to integrate himself and his world; on the other, they serve as the society's most empathic voice, the societal acknowledgement of the reality of inner needs.

The great religions, which were—or aspired to be—total structurings of human group behavior, regulators of psychological, social, political, and economic action, have been reduced to styles of individual or local group therapeutic behavior—a realm of compassion partially set aside from the ordinary spheres of life. The breaking of the human and social container of religious restraints has afforded social and individual scope that is at once our gain and our loss. This loss is in large part the loss of social coherence, and of a structure in which the individual had a clearer idea of his own social space.

The *resonance* of private and public actions is crucial to the maintenance of social safe space. It is crucial for individuals to be able to feel that what they are, or what they at least strive to be, in their private lives has something to do with what they are as members of society. There is a very great difference between Roman Catholic life in medieval Europe, Buddhist life in pre-Communist Tibet, Inca life in pre-Spanish Peru, and the isolated practice of religious morality and ritual as psychological or aesthetic operations in an alien culture. A thread is not a blanket; a refuge or a sub-culture is not the same thing as a clearly structured world. A Buddhist in Manhattan might benefit from the therapeutic of his system—he might even share it in a small group or network—but the rhythms of Manhattan are not those of the temple gong and mountain thunder; and the individual meaning of a philosophical view must undergo change when it represents a private retreat but not a socially confirmed way of life.

In a similar though more subtle way, psychotherapy *as a way of being* finds itself disconnected from a cultural home that would reinforce its values through resonance from educational, aesthetic, and political institutions. In fact, just as religions, art, journalism, and law are threatened by subordination to the state and its propaganda, so is psychiatry often distorted in the service of the state—validating societal failure by identifying dissent, nonconformity, rebellion and breakdown as forms of pathology. Just as journalists in wartime are often self-censoring for fear of being persecuted or from guilt about being unpatriotic, so are we all interfered with in our way of seeing, saying, and being by our Babel of cultural guidelines and vocabularies.

In religious civilization, the ethos was clear, even if perverted by the state—and it always emphasized the sacred space of mutual obligations and individual dependence on the collective social product. Any church symbolizes interdependence. What tended to get lost in social practice was the sacred space of individual development: And so the Buddhists retired to their monasteries, and the Christians paid taxes to Caesar and retired to the next world. Religion became the guardian and the expression of the individual's sense of privacy and meaning, the guardian of inner space, but no longer the guarantor of a safe social world. Religion became the symbol of an unlivable ideal way to live.

The problem of realization remains similar for those who seek to order their experience according to the empathic understanding of psychotherapy: How to protect the space of the human subject in the political space—how to align the inner and outer treasuries. In an era of political reduction of the empathic or religious dimension of experience, psychotherapy faces the task of extending its home range into other institutions, and of seeking to become a regulator of an only partially integrated culture—one containing many religions as medical, legal, and therapeutic groups, each having its own vocabulary. In a schizoid world, each religious group idealizes its own god, and devalues other groups as "heathen" or "barbarian"—not human. Scapegoating interferes with common understanding, as does each group's dread of losing its distinctive identity.

By contrast, the integrative task of psychotherapy as a social movement is to facilitate mutual recognition. Psychotherapy can be seen as the social incarnation of Einstein's theory of general relativity, conserving the positions, identities, and points of view of all groups as transformations of the same humanity. The recognitions of psychotherapy are like those of the great religions—*I am you and you are me*—but its countertheme is *We are separate and individual,* not, as in mistaken ideology, *We are good, you are evil.* The social task of psychotherapy is one of meditation—between parts of the self, generations, sexes, races, religions, therapeutic styles, and social vocabularies. Our cultures divide us less than our fears.

SOCIAL INTEGRATION: BEYOND DENIAL

Social integration does not destroy individuals; it reinforces individuation by a process of resonance and recognition. In this society we are addicted to individual identity understood mainly in the adolescent style of defiance—*I am not you.* Therefore it has become popular to speak of "doing my own thing" with a shrillness unmitigated by a sense of social bonds and mutual responsiveness.

Adolescents must adopt this developmental attitude of self-absorption; and so do rebelling populations if they are being exploited and controlled—but such splitting behavior can be reduced in the empathic social climate of mutual exchange. The adolescent dreads assimilation by the parent, but the empathic adult welcomes recognition and resonance because he understands that we are all on the same path, although our maps and clocks may differ.

Whatever frees us from the yoke of comparison, envy, and life-or-death competition frees us to live in our own moment—the only jewel we can own. This triple jewel of the present moment is clear perception, shared feeling, and understanding of the wheel of change. We all live through the same life cycle. The struggle of every culture is to regulate its ecology in such a way that our real wealth—this clear perception and exchange of feelings—is not subordinated to the nightmare of manic definitions of wealth—the frozen surplus, the fortress, the perpetual killing and dismemberment of rivals, the splitting off and denial of social groups that remind us of our poverty and of our failures.

Just as the individual reintegrates by means of recognition of his own error, weakness, fault, fright, and rage, the society, too, has its own recognitions to go through. The individual denial of responsibility and guilt has its counterpart in the social denial. In recent history we have seen the struggle entailed by the recognition of societal guilt and failure; the social attention focused upon the Kennedy assassination, Vietnam, Watergate, and the secret government of the CIA reflects not only our native love for sensationalism and our economy's feeding on its elaboration, but also the stirrings of an ethical unease. Pollution, racism, sexism, and corporate corruption may no longer be projected so easily onto an external enemy—these problems are ours.

But we deny our social problems even as we recognize them: The ex-President is pardoned even before he is adjudged guilty; and for each citizen who recognizes in the labyrinth of Executive testimony the schizoid defenses of our society and ourselves carried to their natural extreme, there probably is another who makes this commonality an excuse for social evil. *All of us do these things, only we don't get caught,* runs the argument. The empathic view—*I am like you and you are like me*—becomes perverted into a justification of a life without commitment in which promises are meaningless, denial is rampant, betrayal of trust is ubiquitous, and the honest image is only a mask for a monstrously distorted face. The social lie supports the private lie; and a thousand private lies diminish the shock value of public deception.

In a similar way, the nation that mourned Kennedy with such fervor is the same nation whose television screens have showed innumerable visions of less illustrious tragedies. The bloody injuries of Detroit, Chicago, and—night after night, year after year—Vietnam have been flickering images to which the ordinary citizen has known no remedy but to close his eyes, mind, and heart. The phenomenon of non-response, once much-discussed and now a way of life, is the social counterpart of the denial of the individual self and of the individual others close to the self.

The society shapes the family that shapes the individual. There is no surprise, then, in finding that the societal problems are expressed in and through the family, just as the family problems are expressed through the individual. Just as the schizoid mechanism represents the compromise between the family primal scene and the individual's reactions, so the primary social forms represent the biological inheritance of pairing, splitting, and hierarchy as they are mediated by the dominant child-rearing attitudes evolved in family life. Our social forms come to us via a long evolution, from infanticide—in fact as well as in fantasy—through forms of parental intrusion, projection, and control, into the empathic forms for which, ostensibly, we strive today.

Gandhi tried to develop appreciative or empathic forms of social change which minimized projection. Erik Erikson views Gandhi's Satyagraha, or Truth Force, as a lever, mobilizing action potentials inhering in a situation—not by polarizing and scapegoating, but by selecting a focus for action which involves the improvement of position by a social group without violation of the integrity of the repressing group. This is bridgework, operating like the locks of a canal, elevating levels of connection and mutual influence. Such respectful action confronts an adversary through self-suffering and understanding of the truth value of other's position. It is parallel to the developmental leverage of the psychoanalytic transference, which continuously upgrades the pathways of communication from denial and projection to mutual receptivity.

Satyagraha seeks to mobilize the best available potentials of the parties in a confrontation. Our social need is for processes of conflict regulation which reduce the split between action and ideal. Satyagraha, like psychoanalysis, is the transmutation of violence into directed social action which energizes all participants in a respectful, non-antagonistic conflict. Both forms of social leverage accept a locus of action that is limited, concrete, and specific, in order to attempt to create realizations of wider species identity and to overcome scapegoating. They try to extend empathic parenting into wider social realms. Gandhi failed because individuals, families, and nations were not ready to accept mature forms of conflict resolution.

There is a parallel between the brinkmanship of the Cold War era and the non-communicative rage of a depressed family. Uniting nations in more than a rhetorical or formal way depends upon the faith of millions of families that trust is possible. Political relations do not depend upon the unconscious of one leader, but upon the leader as the representative of the psychic stage of development of crucial groups in a population. The psyche reflects the economy. Empathic parental consciousness depends upon surplus—without surplus, exploitative forms emerge.

In an earlier state of social development, inhibition and scarcity of goods and status roles were inherent in social grouping. Both rigid hierarchies and unregulated competition reflect "pre-human" forms of social life. Infanticide, inhibition of individual development, splitting off, caste-formation, expulsion, attack and consumption of surplus or "marginal" animals by predators: All these can be recognized as biological forms of population-regulation. Scarcity of social goods means restricted and always vulnerable space for the self. The process of civilization—of humanizing individual, family, and social relations—is the process of converting this system of inhibition and life-and-death competition into a system which encourages the development of *every* member of society into a full human being with a safe and reliable social space.

In our culture today, a main actor in this process of conversion from a system of inhibition to a system of empathic encouragement of individual growth is the psychotherapist. The psychotherapist uses his or her dominance as a social animal to encourage growth, not to inhibit or exploit the patient. Ideally, this would be the role of parents and of the society. But parents and politicians, unlike psychotherapists and other "helping persons," have only a vacillating commitment to encouraging the growth of *all* members of the group. The same problem plagues the United Nations. It still sanctions inhibition and drastic in-equality, based on real and fantasy scarcity.

EMOTIONAL ORGANIZERS

The political mood of the governing body of the society, or the emotional state or stage of development of the parent in the family, determines what organizes the psyches of the group members. This emotional organizer can vary from terror of emptiness and separation, to scapegoating rage, to security which allows exploration and play. Making conscious the way in which emotional organizers work in family life is the task of psychoanalysis and other forms of psychotherapy. Making conscious the way emotional organizers work in our social life has been, so far, the task of isolated critics.

Our understanding of these emotional organizers is crucial. At stake is whether we are to be crushed as individuals and social beings by the wheel of the life cycle and the succession of generations, or whether we can live out our lives in safety within this process of rotation, at play among its meanings.

Huizinga wrote in *Homo Ludens* that civilization arises in and as play. The conversion of life-and-death-anxiety situations into situations insulated by security is a continuing process. In our social life, war, starvation, disease, crime, and exploitation sustain the psychic forms that freeze the capacity to play. Although the play tendencies in our culture are powerful, expressing themselves through vacations, movies, popular music, and sports, as well as through the fundamental forms of commercial exchange, universal neurosis means that the player must be a social reconstruction, involving high investments of social energy. Either we overwork to get the play privilege, or play becomes work (requiring therapy), or we let "stars" do it for us.

Civility, an empathic attitude toward others, remains an ideal in the sense that it is generally reserved only for safe social spaces, usually local space. The expansion of civility and its extension from one's own community or ethnic group to other human groups is blocked by scapegoating and by the economic and political forms of the social nightmare. The process of the extension of civility is parallel to the process of decentralizing the infantile ego, which makes the world revolve around the self, splits off its bad qualities, and projects them into others. The integration of the world of the psyche and the integration of the social body both depend upon the reduction of such Ptolemaic thinking and feeling. This means that there will be no split between *us* and *them;* all people will be *us,* for we know that, although we are different, we are the same. Everyone experiences and destroys experience in the same ways. All nightmares are one nightmare.

SCAPEGOATING

When we do not accept ourselves, and when we experience the self, not as a creature of a universe and a human life cycle that extends beyond ourselves in space and time, but egocentrically, as the only center around which life can move, then we are trapped in the vicious cycle of denial and projection. What works is *me;* and what does not work must be *outside me,* in that unsafe space—the world of others. The energy that must be devoted to maintaining such a split can be measured by the tenacity with which we hold to the view that a scapegoated child or a scapegoated ethnic group is "bad" and to be rejected. Scapegoating is communication confused with blame and with the expulsion of bad contents. The selection of a scapegoat protects the family unit or the social unit from the danger of discovering that we have "bad" in ourselves which we must work to integrate. Scapegoating always involves the disguised attempt to kill or to inhibit a person or group perceived as a rival. The disguised form—you are bad—masks the denied fear and jealousy—which, paradoxically, often inflates a helpless victim into an imaginary persecutor.

Like scapegoating in the family, racism and war are activities more related to the need to project "bad" contents of the self into an external figure than they are to any objective situation. A scapegoating parent one always explain why the bad child is bad; he can give a long list of bads, which are more reflective of hated aspects of the self than any characteristics in the child. The child is seen to be stupid, hostile, lazy, dirty, weak—a bizarre object compounded of the parents' own wishes and fears. A racial stereotype is constructed of the same projected materials; and each projection has the meaning of impoverishing the humanity of the projector as it denies the humanity of the scapegoat.

Integration, at the social as at the individual level, requires us to live with ambivalence, with competition, with imperfection, with incompleted tasks. The immature personality cannot tolerate ambivalence, and feels it can preserve its good figures—parents, mates, children, fellow ethnics, authorities—only by blackening a target object outside the self or the immediate group.

In his courageous book, *The Psychoanalysis of War,* Franco Fornari shows how unconscious needs work to deny aggression toward the state by splitting off the aggression and projecting it onto an enemy. Hating and killing the enemy becomes the dominant form of preserving and loving the good authorities. This is precisely the form taken by families who focus on a scapegoat in order to avoid attacking every family member.

Scapegoating, like all other forms of splitting, makes both inner and outer space unsafe: The space outside the self is full of danger because enemies are projected there; and the space of the inner self is equally unsafe because, when reality is distorted and denied, thought and feeling threaten this distortion and denial.

We are ambivalent in our relations with others, for we never entirely lose our basic fears of separation, disintegration, attack, emptiness, and loss. In extreme forms, these anxieties interfere with receptivity and with the sexual or creative giving of the self as a whole; they split the self. The resolution of these feelings depends on the development of the sense of a self that can securely contain good, and on the setting of limits for others and for the self. Feeling safe depends on being safe, on living in a social context that satisfies our basic needs: intimacy, protection, recognition, status, reciprocity, creativity.

TOWARD SAFE SOCIAL SPACE

When we take part in societal life, not only with basic unresolved needs and fears but with the aggravated fears and needs of the poorly integrated self, then our relations with others and with the society are distorted. When society promotes immaturity and incomplete integration in its members, the process of growth becomes difficult to conceive and to pursue. A society that confirms our infantilism, our self-indulgence, our addictive needs, our blind aggressions, and our denial of empathy cannot function as it should—as a *container* for these needs and immaturities, holding and channeling feeling for the good of the self and of the group.

The ideal of the Sabbath expressed and institutionalized the need for a containing space which limits the pressure on the self for self-control and self-containment. The Sabbath enabled expression through choral song; it enabled the feeling of being held and socially fed; it offered breathing space. The Sabbath was the religious form of safe space and safe time, freeing the individual from the twin chains of compulsive duty and of impulse.

One secular society offers little of sacred space or of time held sacred to basic human needs. Instead, the society caters to our wants, our impulses, and our whims. Like the elaborate, resentful accommodations of a guilty and unloving parent, the once-affluent society offers up a perpetual series of desserts—perhaps the "just desserts" of seekers for instant gratification—which are supposed to substitute for food. In the society as in the family, more catering signifies less nurture.

In every culture, there is some use of narcotics, based on a sense of life as intolerable because of the lack of adequate nurture. So our own culture has given rise to its appropriate counter-culture, which seeks, in altered states of consciousness, the solution to or escape from the unresolved problems of ordinary consciousness.

The desire to alter one's state of awareness may be motivated by denial or by acceptance. Since the adolescent and the immature adult are oriented toward denial, the states of consciousness prized by them are continuous highs—brought on by sensory overload in multi-media bombardment, by physical speed or risk, by loud music, by sensory or sexual experiment, by drugs, or by states of euphoric relaxation. The desire to blast free of the constraints of the body, the group, and the network of social relationship and to sail free into idealized space is characteristic of the adolescent stage of development. Such manic flights may involve positive moves to explore the map and clock of the body, of relationships, of the social institutions containing the self—in order to find limits. Pushed to extremes, the denial of limits becomes its own limit: exhaustion, isolation, emptiness. The fear of being swallowed by limits gradually oscillates back toward acceptance of support and containment, if only to protect against the dangers of scattering into bits. An adolescent needs to take risks and to search for limits.

If we follow the career of Timothy Leary, high priest of the manic adolescents of the 1960s, we see how easily exploration can lead to limitless revolt, and how manic distortions can simplify the complex process of change in individuals and societies. Leary, understandably bored with Harvard academic psychology, came to believe that turning on person after person would lead to a critical segment of the population tuning in on their inner lives and dropping out of the dreamworld of roles and institutions in order to become psychedelic revolutionaries.

Coffee may be made instantly, and fantasy percolates even faster—but neither people nor institutions transform because of one experience. Leary, like all people in manic states, confused experiences with structures. This is precisely the problem of the manic state: It cannot contain awareness of the whole process of the self, its interactions, and its network. Ironically, while Leary caricatured the role of guru, the advertising business began marketing the psychedelic revolution as a consumer product. But the triple world of social roles, family circle, and individual growth is not significantly affected by euphoric moments. Persecuted by the authorities he pronounced unreal, Leary became increasingly enmeshed in intrigue, ending in jail and trying to trade his soul by bargaining for clemency in exchange for betraying former colleagues in the psychedelic underworld.

Leary's career symbolizes any manic revolution. It begins in self-rejection, proceeds through rejection of the given world, and it ends in despair. Adolescent mysticism and Messianic sects share with drug highs a distortion of the map of social worlds and the clock of social change.

However, this does not mean that psychedelic or mind-manifesting drugs or marijuana lack social value. Manic misuse of automobiles does not negate the value of automobiles. Inner exploration may certainly be facilitated by the regulated use of LSD, mescaline, hashish, and other consciousness-altering drugs—just as it may be facilitated by meditation or by psychotherapy. The right use of these three paths all leads toward the clarification of projections in consciousness, the purification of awareness, the opening of the heart to empathy, and the opening of the mind to the laws of structure and transformation. The terrors of bad trips, nightmares, and meditation-hallucinations are all products of projection, of dissociation and the failure to recognize and accept aspects of the self which appear as alien monsters outside the self.

The right way to evaluate the *use* of drugs, alcohol, or other forms of consciousness alteration is to assess their power to integrate the personality and clarify projection—as opposed to dissociating the personality and increasing projection. We are all familiar with the adolescent who solves all his problems on a midnight high, and then fails to awake the next morning. We also have met the clam-like intimidated male who avoids facing any problems until, full of beer, he explodes at his wife, full of fury and resolve which, sadly, leaks away like urine.

Mature adults may have experiences through the use of psychedelic drugs which are similar to those produced in the psychoanalytic transference or in advanced levels of meditation. Such experiences may range from seeing hallucination in action—the visual process of mapping the mother's face onto the wife's and not perceiving the wife separate from this projection—to experiencing time slowing down as the body relaxes, and opening up a whole world of radiant patterns of sound, color, and form. Whether or not these perceptual and emotional frame shifts are integrated into the personality immediately, they offer the experience of a higher power of receptive resolution of the self—*a deeper penetration into experience.*

Sometimes, a psychedelic experience will simply make manifest the person's state of experience. This means that if a person is tense, depressed, and squashed, he will experience this feeling of being crushed in all the bones, sinews, and muscles of his being as agony. This is why psychedelic experience is highly risky, except in the presence of a therapeutic guide who can help the person understand gaps or transitions in understanding his modes of experiencing.

Freud, himself a cigar addict, pointed out that few human beings can bear the stress of living in a complex, repressive society without reliance on a narcotic. The widespread appeal of marijuana rests in its effectiveness in inducing a state of relaxation which resensitizes the body and opens some doors to physical and verbal play. Sometimes, smoking marijuana enables a person to identify "safe" as a feeling of relaxation and low anxiety—a feeling perhaps never before encountered by the person. This is perhaps the most brutal comment on our civilized state: that we need a dream of safety to protect us against a nightmare of routine stress. For many people, the sacred zone of safety—once protected by the gods—has now shrunk to the size of a bag of marijuana or shot of heroin.

The insight of any path of development is that one cannot use one addiction against another, one fixation against another, one attachment against another, one manic state against the totality of experience. Feeling safe means letting go of clinging to ideas, images, anxieties, parts of the self, and parts of the world as if they were magic idols. The only security we can know lies in the process of separation, emptiness, and clarification of confusion and projection which enables self-acceptance and intimacy, and which conducts love and connects us to the powers of shared group life. Safe means fed, warm, held, rhythmic, and *involved.*

The basic helpful alteration in consciousness is the reduction of fear of one's own projections. This opens compassion for the self and empathic and aesthetic appreciation of others. This safe space of seeing, feeling, and understanding humanizes interactions and opens warmth and love.

Any act or substance that stimulates projection is vivid, because it reveals self. But we must be warned that projections cannot be derealized without first being recognized, and that this is a process pervaded by terror. Our basic fear is fear of the biological unconscious. All religions wisely revere and fear their demons, and no person should open Pandora's Box without first securing selfhood. A secure self can face a nightmare sure of the waking. A depressed adolescent swallowing an unknown pill has no such security.

Dr. Thomas Szasz has argued that the "drug abuse problem" is a form of scapegoating. All cultures sanction good substances and taboo bad substances, independent of their physiological effects. Often, this institutionalizes a good/bad confusion and makes shitfood the social norm—as alcohol, sugarfood, and carcinogens. This irrational institutionalization of splitting merely serves to divide societies into good, economically powerful priests and rulers, and non-conforming, exploited victims of their projections. Addicts of all kinds, as we have argued, are primarily people who lack nurturing pair, group, and network relationships. The drug problem is a people problem, a product of any society that normalizes isolation.

As we have shown, therapy can enable an individual to overcome addiction as a state of being, securing and clarifying inner and outer maps and clocks so that objects emerge into clarity, and interactions become personal in scale. But the social institutions that function on the level of addiction inhibit the development of human selves. Social shitfood consists not only of chemical pollution of the environment, but also of scapegoating ideologies, addictive imagery, and non-empathic forms of education—the reduction of human beings to objects.

SAFE SPACE FOR THE GROWING SELF

The primary social problem has always been the appropriate or just distribution of goods. Plato's myth of gold, silver, and bronze castes, like Buddha's metaphor of the universal rain that is absorbed by shrubs, trees, and grass according to differential need, is a classical attempt to conceive the problem. More dynamic is the American Indian conception of the Medicine Wheel, the psychoanalytic view of the life cycle, the Buddhist conception of the Great Vehicle of the Lotus Sutra, and the Marxist view of justice as: from each according to ability, to each according to need. The problem here is one of parallax, of conflicting generational, ethnic, or class positional points of view. Justice is conceivable only through the social clarification of the meaning of wealth or goods, and the pathways of access to them.

Safe space for development at every stage of the life cycle is the basic human need. Present social logic sacrifices real and psychic safe space to the nightmare of the schizoid mechanism. Secret government by fantasy—in the family, in organizations, in nations—means cyclic repetition of the same projective behavior. Conscious government means recognition of needs, fantasies, limits, support, and suffering as they change during the phases of the life cycle.

Our tendency in social life continues to sacrifice marginal people—the helpless, the young, the old, the strangers, the weak—to the needs of the central group, and to make the surplus available to those who need it least. A contrary tendency is the distribution of the surplus according to need—the extension of safe space and goods. Many social inventions, from the Homeric idea that a strange guest might be a god in disguise, or that he is protected by a god, to the holy child, and to the idea of sanctuary, are extensions of the domain of safe space as an outer and inner domain free of fear, insulated from primitive destructive mechanisms.

Civilization is not secure unless it means not only the progressive inhibitions foreseen by Freud in *Civilization and Its Discontents,* but also progressive expressiveness of all levels and modes of human being. This expressiveness consists not of acting out—through murderous feuds, wars, slavery, piracy, child abuse, robbery—but of theatricalized forms and expanded realms of play. Art, leisure, and constructive communal roles are essential to our appropriate, humanized ownership of the forms of violence, greed, envy, competition, scapegoating, and self-destruction, forms which we inherit from more armored generations.

Group life, like individual life, is ambivalent. The group must generate a genius to regenerate the group and help it to be more responsive and adaptive to changing conditions. However, as in the individual, conservative counterforces resist change and tend to inhibit and interfere with change agents. Many situational facts, such as age, sex, class position, and identification, influence how individuals orient toward changes in group norms, codes, and goals. Group life, like individual life, undergoes phase changes, often amidst violent splitting and conflict. The resolution of phase change in new social forms reflects the psychic organization of critical individuals or masses of critical individuals in accordance with the basic paradigms of W. R. Bion's three group forms (pairing, splitting, dependence hierarchy) as they are mediated by progressive changes in the parent-child experience.

Tyranny and infanticide coincide; so do anarchy and the adolescent exploitation of parents; and so do justice and the sense of mutual obligation between generations. The conflicts of our psycho-social period are clearly mirrored in the dilemmas of our Juvenile and Family Court system: the intended extension of empathy to children in programs for prevention of child abuse, the confusion about setting limits for exploitative and destructive adolescents. We must face the reality that one quarter of all American children are being programmed to fail—because of inadequate parenting, schooling, and social resources. Increasing guilt about the care of the elderly is also characteristic of our period. New networks are being built to replace kinship groups, which are decaying.

The mutilation of the individual by the group, or the sacrifice of a part of the individual space in exchange for fear-modification and acceptance of the group clock and map—can only be reduced by an integral system of care-giving that furnishes resonance for each position in the life cycle, from birth to dying. A human life requires pairing, stimulation from a primary group, safe but challenging forms of competitive display, and participation in a hierarchy that connects the self to other networks in the society. Such a conscious system of caring represents the conversion of basic biological strategies of group survival into a process of humanization.

The hard reality is that uncared-for adults are child-neglecting parents and scapegoating citizens. The child is, indeed, father to the man. (The deeper dimension of this problem—the animal is mother to the child—we reserve for a future study.) The psychotherapist works with a group animal in semi-isolation from the group, with the pair form dominant. From this perspective, the psychotherapist exposes and supports unmet needs for nurture, display, aggression, and desire—and, in the crucible of the transference, the psychotherapist matures the individual, enabling the inner and outer expansion of safe, defensible, network-affiliated space. But the network must be realized at every stage of development—or else there is regression toward the nonempathic modes of functioning characteristic of mistrust and life-or-death anxiety. Safe space is a process of continuous recreation and renewal of nurturing networks.

The idealized therapist is the partial incarnation of the empathic ideal which for most children was simply a religious idea or image never realized by hard-pressed parents or teachers. The therapist enables the discovery of compassion—of care for one's own inner organs—extended then to the whole self and finally to others perceived as wholes. But such a path—which was once restricted to the afterlife, to monasteries, or to sacred zones of time and space—is now beginning to develop as an empathic network—like early systems of transportation and communication, or like a new form of religion.

The integrated individual in a safe, empathic network is the paradigm for the care-giving society, resonant with the growth of all and each. The subordination of violence to law and law to care is the promise of religion. The practice of religion is the self-development of each person in groups and networks which empathize with the all-sided development of each member. This condition is the end of history as a nightmare and the beginning of human history—the return of the gods to earth in human form. Incarnations, avatars, or heroes all have the same task—whether they are called Hercules, Odysseus, Beowulf, Buddha, Jesus, Mohammed, or Moses. The task is clearly stated in the Hindu epic, *The Ramayana*. The purpose of Rama's incarnation is to encounter and destroy demons and monsters who cause suffering and hardship to good people; he seeks to abolish fear from the heart and to make safe space for peace, gentleness, beauty, and justice. Every people has its own struggle and seeks a psychic and social form of redemption from the nightmare: a god.

FROM INHIBITION TO EMPATHY

The argument of this book is that safe space for feeling depends, not upon money, power, or control but upon the capacity to be involved with a pair, with groups, and with social networks which enable one to feel known, loved, recognized, and constructive. Feeling safe is this process of being held in productive giving and receiving relationships with others. This process is the only process that can modulate guilt and reduce depression. Let us remember that guilt is the feeling of not doing enough, or of doing damage, or of being unable to love. It is also a feeling produced when others envy our aliveness and act injured in order to inhibit us. Guilt either paralyzes creativity or overdrives it, as long as a person feels insecure in the process of giving and receiving. The pair, group, and network, if they resonate in empathic ways, can secure the goodness of the self as a daily process of mutuality. When a person is not securely held by daily interchanges with empathic persons, projection begins to challenge perception and integration. We require constant renewal of our maps, and constant tuning of our clocks. We are social animals.

Guilt is a process of equilibration. If a person wants to have more than he or she is willing to pay for in terms of the social process of giving for what is received, on some level this person will be unable to have or to enjoy what is wished for or possessed. Guilt ensures that, when mutual obligations are not respected, the exploiter pays. However, unconscious guilt also is a mechanism of inhibition and suppression, making individuals and whole social groups feel that their gifts are poor and that they do not deserve to have social goods. If children, women, ethnic groups, or manual laborers feel that their gifts are inferior, they also are inhibited in their capacity to feel safe enough to give and to receive love.

Feeling safe means having clear objects, and knowing that others are like oneself—undergoing all the stages of development from birth to dying. Clear perception of the giving and receiving rhythms and of the products of these different stages of development enables us to participate safely in all relationships. Feeling unsafe means that the nightmare interferes in our perception of ourselves, others, and social forms, and that we then become unsure of what we see, feel, give, and receive.

Because we are transitional between an inhibitive and empathic social organization, we are often uncertain as persons, as families, and as citizens in society, about whether we are paranoid or whether we are being persecuted. The family and the government, as well as our large corporations, give the same double message and produce the same knot of fear and doubt. The double message is: *We love you and want you to grow—but there is no room for you, no time for you, no understanding of your specific needs.* The double message is: *You are a subject, you have a precious soul, your inner wealth is your feelings—but we must treat you like an object.* Whenever we encounter this situation, we are likely to become confused and disoriented. Our parents, our governing institutions—our stars to navigate by—appear to be moving in one direction, and yet they are going in another direction. We are being dismembered, and even our confusion and disorientation is not remembered.

Denial and ideology serve the same function, conserving and obscuring injustice. Only a system of justice rooted in empathy can afford to be transparent. *Clear* is one of our metaphors for *safe*. When we are clear about our families and our social institutions, we may not feel good about them, but we will not feel the violence and the guilt produced by denial and distortion.

Because we are products, in our first incarnation, of families acting as agents of the social nightmare, the schizoid mechanism and defensive armoring shape our unsafe way of being. What has been called rebirth, in religious and therapeutic contexts, is untying the knots of this process and coming to trust our own perceptions of family and of social process. The first step in this process of rebirth is compassion for those knots in the self, for the double track that interferes with our experience. The second step is generally acting out our rage at the violent distortion of our selves. This process is safely done by the individual in psychotherapy. There, the therapist as an empathic container can help us find ourselves and repair our connections to our feelings.

However, in the social arena, much of the acting out is done by groups in power, and there is no container. There is no working through, only an endless repetition of the same forms of scapegoating, control games, war games, infanticide, genocide, and mutilation. This process produces a schizoid feeling in our educators and social workers. They are presumably committed to individual growth and development; and yet they cannot serve the children or the deprived families entrusted to them because the logic of the institutions they serve is more attuned to the social nightmare than to the clock of client development. How can teachers communicate information, security, cooperativeness, and courage when they are themselves terrified of losing their jobs and of being scapegoated by budget-cutting school boards? No one can give what he or she does not have.

The paradox of our culture is that we require empathic behavior from our parents, our teachers, our social workers, and our citizens without affording them enough nurture, security, and community to enable them to develop into an empathic position. This holds true even though it is a common understanding that empathy is a developmental position that must be constructed—a position of surplus and generosity. This demand that deprived individuals behave in empathic ways reinforces a tendency toward splitting and scapegoating. It reinforces denial in parents and teachers, as well as in the unemployed or the marginally employed. They must blame someone for failing to achieve an ideal form of giving which depends on a security that they have never been offered.

Politics is a kind of balance of blame system, a system of exploitation and repression based in expediency rather than in an understanding of the needs of different groups or different generations, based in a secure set of empathic priorities. Being "realistic" generally turns out to mean blaming the victim, and exploiting and inhibiting the weaker group to serve the interests of a controlling group. The problem with this form of behavior in parents or governments is that it perpetuates itself through repetition. We do what is done to us, instead of learning from our experience. It has often been said that what we learn from history is that we do not learn from history. Learning means facing the mechanisms of denial, splitting, and projection both in our families and in our governing social bodies.

Szasz has argued that "mental illness" is also a form of scapegoating, similar to witch-hunting. We have considered juvenile delinquency, crime, and war to be similar forms of disguised scapegoating or splitting—involving projection from one group of the social body upon another member or group. A safe society is one which reduces all forms of projection and scapegoating, substituting appreciation—appreciation of every person's struggle to grow a human self—for devaluation and inflation. Without nurture, recognition, and status, and limits, we would all be potentially "mentally ill," delinquent, criminal, and warlike. The reader of this book is the product of a vast social investment—of capital, protein, information, and attention.

The basis of the social and psychic nightmare is the infanticidal, persecutory, and inhibitive practice and fantasy of deprived adults against children at all ages, but especially in infancy and during adolescence. These practices and fantasies derive from biosocial population control mechanisms. The feelings of life-and-death competition with siblings and with everyone are products of a pre-human social mechanism for regulating numbers and status roles. On this level, to be marginal, vulnerable, nonconforming, or weak is to be menaced by mutilation. We know that child-neglecting and child-abandoning parents are themselves not only deprived, but also the agents of social messages which mean: no food, no space, no growth, no love—die. Psychosis and neurosis are products of this social winnow. Much of social space is still pervaded by life-or-death competition, or the threat of destruction and exclusion. In safer social spaces, the fantasies persist, the projections persist, and the life-and-death anxiety persists. We call this "neurosis."

VIOLENCE AND RESONANCE IN GROUP LIFE

All the paranoid fantasies and nightmares are real *on some* level—as biological modes, as historical practices, and as fantasies of others transmitted through posture, gesture, and a full range of symbolic communication signals. Our problem is both the politics of these threatening gestures as well as the reaction-formation in the individual psyche which becomes character armor, the schizoid mechanism, continuous projection, and the barrier to empathy. Social violence produces regressive resonance in the individual—as "pre-human" behavior and fantasy.

Documentation for this position may be found readily in Wynne-Edwards, *Animal Dispersion in Relation to Social Behavior* and in the *History of Childhood Quarterly*. The psychoanalytic writings providing the linkage between animal behavior and the modes of human fantasy are those of Melenie Klein, although she herself did not make this connection.

W. R. Bion, in *Experiences in Groups,* began to connect the modes of group behavior to unconscious fantasy. When in groups, we automatically and unconsciously try to form pairs, fighting groups, or dependence hierarchies.

There is nothing "wrong" with such behavior: Pairing is the basis of sexual reproduction, marriage, and child-nurture. And just as splitting or fighting is the basis of politics, dependence hierarchy is the basis of corporate organizational forms. All of these forms correspond to appropriate work tasks if a person has experienced pairing, splitting, or dependence in empathic forms in family life. If not, a person is unable to concentrate very long in *any* work task without falling into seductive, antagonistic, or passive-dependent behavior in ways that interfere with group life—whether the group is a family, a learning group, or a production group. We have all experienced ourselves and others paralyzed in our group behavior by one person behaving in a seductive, factionalizing, or infantile way. Group work is constantly interrupted by persons who shout, *Look at me!* or *You are bad—I'm leaving,* or *Feed me, Feed me.* Sometimes these three forms are all that is going on in an immature marriage. Sometimes a group gets stuck in scapegoating and loses its understanding of social goals. Very often, we are simply suffering confused group life because these unconscious forms interrupt us in our attempts to assert ourselves, care for a group, or solve a social problem.

The display behavior involved in seduction is part of an ancient mating game, and it is related to many social rituals. Males compete with aggressive social threat gestures in order to achieve a social status space and to secure a fascinating mate. This dominance behavior insures that the male has enough power to overcome the resistances of the female and then to support the social space necessary to raise a family. The struggle to achieve a status space goes on within each generation and between generations. In nature, the struggle is a life-or-death struggle—for a humiliated animal is a defenseless animal.

Problems of violence are widespread and basic. They include categories of interference expressed in Buckminster Fuller's patterns of real converging vectors: displacement, dismembering, bending, collision, and orbital entrainment. The basic parasitic-host forms of devouring, castration, and disease express the competition for protein and space in the microbiotic field. Alleochemics, or chemical ecology, reveals that many actions of attack, defense, and avoidance involve chemical agents rather than physical force. On all levels, in all modes, violence means positional conflict.

Collective social violence is normal in the sense that it—or the threat of force—is involved in any basic realignment of positions of power, whether national or international. Violence is used in defence of positions near the Good by those holding the means of production; it is used against those in positions of class power in the name of justice; and it may be used by the middle class against both top and lower levels in fear of the loss of a good position. The basic forms of collective violence are signs of the nature of the social and political process, and of changes in that process. This holds for clan feuds, religious schism, strikes, and riots. Violence is often viewed through the metaphor of voice. Therapy and empathic forms of social conflict enable more people to have a voice, and reduce violence, or socialize its expression in constructive ways.

The forms of violence in the individual are also basic indicators of process: Rage, violence, auto-toxicity, modulated anger, hate and creative aggression have positional developmental meaning and value. Our social task is to reduce denial, random violence, splitting, and projection, and to encourage empathic forms of conflict and aggression.

A humanized society educates each person to productively participate in pair, group, and network forms so that persons may develop the capacity for love, legitimate conflict, leadership, dependence, support, and the possibility of empathic understanding of the suffering of others in their various stages in the life cycle and positions in group life. The freezing of a group, or of any part of a group in *one mode,* dismembers the people in that group, whether women are frozen in a posture of seduction or nurture, or men are frozen in a posture of warfare, or children and adolescents are frozen in a posture of helpless dependence.

A whole person is one who can safely relate to his body, his pairs, his groups, and his networks—protected not only by the law but also by empathic institutions which are not designed to kill, control, persecute, or dismember, but which allow for phases of expansion and integration of every person. The guideline of such an empathic society is the same in the ideal Christian, Buddhist, and Marxist commonwealth—from each according to his powers, to each according to his needs. In the governing schizoid group forms, the formula remains: to each according to his power, from each according to his fears. The social body of depression continues to govern and inhibit the empathic person.

Just as we must struggle against the nightmare governing our waking hours, so we must struggle against the schizoid mechanism governing our emotional behavior, and against the biological forms of group life which threaten to dominate our political life. The same shadow is over all the forms of our experience—emptiness, mutilation, starvation, and domination by the excremental deposits of past generations. When we open our eyes to this nightmare as adults, we are not terrified, but determined; and we need to begin repairing the damage done by historical and fantasy behavior—our own deeds, and our inheritance. The sun of democracy does not rise without our aid from the doom of Buchenwald.

We must use all the power of our sexuality, all the cunning of our warmaking ability, all the conductive capability if the hierarchy, in order to reverse the wheel of exploitation, to give no additional inch to death or death-in-life. When our eyes and hearts are open, we become lions of the law, tigers of empathy. Subject to no nightmare, suffering through our own schizoid mechanism, refusing to participate in forms of domination and scapegoating—neither victim nor victimizer—we stand in a clear light of justice and empathy, and of mutual obligation between individuals and generations, giving and receiving from out positions of support—our pairs, our groups, our networks—flashing signs of recognition, eye to eye, weaving the fabric of new social forms.

Once, only heroes descended into underworlds to emerge in forms of redemptive power. Now, through forms of individual and group therapy, many thousands of people are emerging, blinking from the shadows. As we close ranks and recognize each other, the monsters that are no monsters but projections of our own selves, in our personal, social, and political lives, begin to go the way of dinosaurs. Resonance is crucial to the maintenance of all our forms of consciousness as well as our social forms—regressive as well as progressive.

THE THREE TIER SYSTEM

We secure our identity through having good reflections and good giving and receiving with intimate pairs—with a parent, mate, child, friend, or a therapist in a repairing relationship. Such pairs help us to accept interactions with a primary group of family members or friends, as well as to accept a work group. Full support for the self then extends to the network—church, social organization, extended family, political party, union, or other group which offers linkages in the local community. Such a three-tier system offers a safe map and a safe clock for local space; it is a resonant system of support in which each level offers compensations or reinforcements for the changes in the other levels. For example, the loss of a loved parent or mate can be compensated for by the intensification of the interaction with the primary group or the network, so that empty space is minimized during a period of loss, and understanding and repair are maximized.

If we are not held by involvement in the present, we cling to the past on an inner track, isolating ourselves.

This formulation of the need for the pair, the primary group, and the network implies two problems. First, the pair, the primary group, and the network may offer security at the cost of a good/bad confusion that inhibits the self; what is identified as "good" by the group may be bad for the individual, while "good" for the individual may be seen as "bad"—as a threat to the stability of the group. Second, we do not live in a social system that is responsive to personal needs. Government, banking, media, and corporate production constitute a national and international network which is alienating and as difficult to regulate as the unconscious. All we are saying here is that the minimum condition of social individual well-being is the presence of such a three-tier system of stimulation. The dissolution of the extended family *as* the three tier system in a traditional culture is a challenge to create new "safe" social forms.

Safe space presents us with three parallel problems—the unconscious, the family, and the social body. The regulation of the projections of the social body are similar to the problem of the regulation of unconscious fantasy. Each involves problems of recognition and of the power to change. As we describe in *Trusting Yourself,* inner power to change depends upon the use of the therapist as a lever, a feedback system, an amplifier; and similarly, the power to induce social change depend upon some parallel regulatory system. Although we can confidently predict that progress in therapy will mean a better relation to the self, to a pair, to a primary group, and to a local network—it does not follow that such progress will have an impact on racism, war, inflation, crime, or other bad dreams of the social body.

THE PSYCHE AND THE SOCIAL BODY

The nightmare of the nuclear world of the psyche is the same as the nightmare of the social body. The family lie is the same as the social lie. The corrective recognition of the family lie through therapy is not matched by any parallel social institution. Much of group life consists of a self-confirming delusion, just as family life consists of a self-confirming delusion. The insight that the nightmares of the individual and of the social body are the same has *almost* been formulated three times—once by Marx, once by Darwin, and once by Freud.

In his notebooks, Darwin grappled with the problem of his own dreams as part of the problem of comprehending the link between animal and human worlds. Similarly, Marx, who often conceived of the world of capital as a dreamlike world of human beings alienated from their emotional powers and turned into objects, tried to make one language for grasping social and emotional process. Freud, who showed that dreams and projections are more "real" than apparent objects or facts, also tried to formulate civilization as a set of illusions that masked the social work of repression of sexual and aggressive energy.

Wilhelm Reich was the first to try to struggle with these three disparate ways to understand the social dream and the individual dream; he was driven toward grandiosity and paranoia by his inability to tolerate or to communicate his understanding of the agony of social sexual economy. Since his time, W. R. Bion's research into the forms of group life, and the development of psychohistorical analysis, has offered us new ways to see and understand social behavior.

Most recently, animal ethology and sociobiology have made contributions toward clarifying the nature of the ego as a body ego, the self as an animal self, the social world as an animal world, and the psychology of the self in a biosocial world. The more we allow our dream—our repressed past—into our consciousness, the more we free ourselves from constraint. What we can see we can change; what we cannot see governs us in secret ways—in our emotional as well as our social life. We shall reserve for another book discussion of the evolutionary basis of the self, focusing here on the alignment of our understanding of the psychic dream to illuminate the social dream.

Group life involves the mutilation of the individual. This fact is a fantasy; this fantasy is a fact. It is hard to look at a nightmare, or at the blinding face of the god that organizes group life. But safe space is not to be found in the forms of flight or withdrawal. Inside the nightmare, we will find the path out of delusion. What we found in the psyche—attack, dread of emptiness, mutilation fantasies, envy, spite, inhibition, greed, splitting, denial, projection, and the dread of guilt—we find also in the social form. Of course, such forms are found in the psyche because they are biosocial forms. When individuals awaken from the psychic forms of life-and-death anxiety about being eaten, mutilated, reabsorbed into mother's body, expelled, emptied out, drained, starved, or humiliated by competition and inhibition, we discover ourselves to be surrounded, not simply by other individuals trapped in this cave of illusion, but by social and political forms which confirm the reality of the illusion.

The need to escape this hellish situation has produced many forms of monastic withdrawal, or otherworld illusions, messianic political sects, narcotic addictions, and social rationalizations of the exploitations of the many by the few. As in therapy, there is no magic, and words must not be confused with social action. Christ formulated social phase change in terms of redemptive transformation in the Second Coming. Marx formulated it through the action of a revolutionary party as a superconducting agent of change. Both are theories of resonance and are full of hope. But the problems of social resonation were not clearly understood; and manic ideas of change remain more dominant than socially and individually integrated changes. The church and the political party remain partially in the dream they seek to awaken from, as do schools which ignore the empathic basis of learning.

The safe space developed by an individual inside the self is a product of the relation between the self and its own childhood, as well as between the self and its past and present relationships to the pair, the groups, and the networks sustaining the self. This safe space is the limit of the freedom and empathy of the self. Simply expressed, the ability of the self to accept its own animality and its own childhood and adolescent needs is the clock and the map of behavior. The more restricted a person's identification with the self, the more restricted is his field of emotional and social flexibility. Self-rejection is the feeling of no time and no space, no empathy for the self, and no empathy for others. Self-acceptance opens us to the richest variety of rhythms and the most varied territory.

PSYCHOHISTORY AND THE HISTORY OF CHILDHOOD

Earlier, we tried to express how the schizoid mechanism keeps the self locked into a track running parallel with the past. Most recently, support for this view of human behavior has emerged from the group publishing the journal titled *History of Childhood*. Lloyd de Mause, editor of the book *The History of Childhood,* begins, "The history of childhood is a nightmare from which we have only recently begun to awaken." The thesis of this important book is that as we go further back in history, we find lower and lower levels of empathic child care. While one could quarrel with the periodization of different forms of child care as an historical scheme involving distinct dates of transition, there is no question that there has been an historical progression in the dominant forms of child care, and that each era experiences its psychological and political space in terms of the dominant forms of child care.

The six stages discriminated by this psychohistory group are: the infanticidal mode of antiquity, the abandonment mode (4th to 13th century), the ambivalent mode (14th to 17th century), the intrusive mode (18th century), the socialization mode (19th to mid-20th century), and the helping mode (mid-20th century). The evidence that infanticide and abandonment was pervasive in earlier historical periods is overpowering, as is the magnitude of the denial practiced by historians. Similarly, there is powerful evidence of continuing forms of depersonalizing intrusion and control of children's bodies and minds. Parents are still not educated to be parents. It is only recently that the child has become in favored households not only free of violent physical and sexual abuse but also free of being used as a toilet or garbage can for parental hostility or self-hate, or as a breast to nurture immature parents. Only recently have we produced adults with enough empathic relation with their own inner feelings from the past to respond with empathy or flexibility to the regressive needs of children. In fact, in some ways we have created new conflicts in mothers and fathers who expect themselves to empathize with their children and who feel guilty about not doing so, but who cannot because they have no empathy for the self.

How we are treated as children determines the way we relate to our self, and our self-relation determines our relation to others. If we are threatened with death and abandonment and are physically abused, we identify with such behavior and project it onto others. But now there is a triple track, not just a double track. Not only does the parent enact the experience of childhood, but the political forms also sanction and reflect the parental forms. The state kills, abandons, and abuses, confirming the reality of the delusion of the parents who are struggling to express or control such remembered behavior. The child was a scapegoat; the parent is a scapegoater; the state scapegoats.

The child has always been associated in fantasy with excrement and with the devil, as well as with food. The child is a product of the projective system of the parents, loaded with their denials and frustrated wishes. Such a child grows up to reproduce such behavior as a parent, surrounded by parallel social forms: the scapegoating of blacks, Jews, Catholics, Arabs, hippies—all shit, all devils, all incarnating parts of the self compounded of dread and erotic fantasies of power. The forms of the nightmare wash over the self in waves; solid land turns to waves and the sky wheels over. The resonance of the nightmare echoes through all our social forms.

It is usual for writers struggling here at the edge of the tolerable to invoke Shakespeare for confirmation and dramatic clarification. And it is appropriate for us, as survivors of world wars who are trying to emerge into a world of reconciliation and philosophical comedy, to reach, not for tragedy, but to Shakespeare's late romance, *A Winter's Tale*, which turns tragedy into comedy, reconciling winter and spring.

In this drama, a king is entertaining his best friend. Suddenly, mistrust, based upon a regressive identification with his young son, clouds the king's mind. He projects a paranoid fantasy upon his wife and friend, believing that she has betrayed him and that his friend is the father of his new baby. He imprisons his wife, tries to kill his friend, exposes his baby to death, and separates his son from his mother, causing the son to die. In the grip of his paranoid fantasy, the king pronounces the wonderfully ambiguous judgment that *all that is true is mistrust.*

When trust is mistrust, tyranny is the social form, and scapegoating is the message. In the immature mind and in immature social forms, ideals turn into devils. In a dialogue with the queen, the king, who has become a victim of nightmares, accuses the queen of actions which cause nightmares. She responds that his dreams have produced her actions. The world is his projection. Any criminal could say what the queen says: The incestuous fantasy of the king creates the social forms of nightmares. Remember Richard Nixon, the White Knight, protector of the faithful against the reds, the blacks, and the lawbreakers? Mistrust was his truth, served by denial and projection. Killing, betrayal, control, and lying still resonate through our social forms.

In the *Winter's Tale,* the truth of mistrust is replaced by the truth of recognition, guilt, and grief—and much is then repaired. Empathy emerges and the warring generations inside the king and among his subjects are reconciled and harmonized. Shakespeare dramatizes the interaction between the child, the man, and the political form in such a way that we can see the memory—the nightmare of childhood—become social fact, overpowering the real facts and the voice of the gods. Our critical social dilemma is that we lack social forms other than the pair form of psychotherapy in which to enact the necessary dramas of projection, recognition, grief, and correction—so that many of our real social forms, including the educational and judicial systems, are constructed largely of social projections which are as self-confirming as the king's dream of betrayal.

In *Life is a Dream,* by Calderon de la Barca, a king imprisons his own son because of a fantasy that his son will kill him. The son is raised in isolation like a dangerous beast, and he is full of rage at the father. So when the father tests the son, raising him to kingship overnight, then, as if in a dream, the son goes berserk, confirming the father's fantasy of a murderous child. The king then jails his son. The instant loss of his omnipotence convinces him that life is a dream and that social roles are evanescent. In a parable of maturation that reminds one of Sufi and Buddhist stories, the prince renounces revenge and power as motives, because they are delusions, and he embraces empathy and the code of virtuous action for its own sake. In both *A Winter's Tale* and *Life is a Dream,* there is the notion of the second and third chance to resolve the problem of repetition of the infantile trauma of dismemberment, rejection, inhibition, being intruded into, being controlled, and its reversal and repetition in the dream of omnipotent power and control. As we move through the different stages of the life cycle and into the different stages of pairs, groups, and networks, we have the opportunity to recognize ourselves and others in a more empathic way. This flexibility dethrones the schizoid mechanism—in certain individuals.

In individual development and in the evolution of parent-child forms, there is the possibility of regressing to earlier stages and suffering them through the second time around. Whatever is denied and not suffered is repeated. Sometimes, a parent can learn to play by playing with a child, even if his or her parent never played with him or her as a child. Parenting involves a complex mirroring process, and the parent, like the political form, and like the patient in psychoanalysis, evolves successively deeper empathic identifications through accepting more and more of the stages of suffered experience. Just as safe space consists of this expanded empathic domain of suffered experience, so unsafe space is defined by the limits of adult anxiety tolerance when confronted by infantile forms of helplessness, which are denied and excluded. The redemption of history from nightmare is this progressive opening of the childhood experience and progressive subjectifying of the falsely "objective" domain of institutions which cannot remember childhood except as an identification with persecutory, rejecting, judgmental, controlling, and dependent parents—parents lacking empathic recognition. To the extent that any group does not remember the suffering of childhood, to that extent the group dismembers and mutilates its members.

Powerful formulations of the path of empathy may be found in the Buddhist canon. Buddha taught the cost of error and the profit of empathy. There are many other parallel formulations of the ideal of empathy, including the New Testament, the American Indian conception of the Medicine Wheel, the Jewish mystical tradition, the alchemic mystical tradition, the Sufi way of wisdom, and the psychoanalytic tradition. All healing traditions converge on the power of empathy channeled through the amplifier of understanding. The goal is the maturation of all creatures. The sage or bodhisattva in this tradition is the one who overcomes ignorance and anxiety about the self, and who comes to understand the needs and modes of human beings and all other creatures through an empathic receptive vision. Because the healer has no need to exploit others with this information, he or she is free to help other human beings with appropriate maturational gifts. These gifts include: material things, kind words, beneficial actions, warmth, understanding, energy, and consistency between words and deeds. Such giving is designed to keep the receiver on the path of development. The giving reflects the attunement of the healer to the developmental limits of the person suffering from ignorance and deprivation. The powers of such giving reside in their harmonization with the needs of the recipient and their synchronization with the field of growth surrounding the recipient. The healer gives only what can be received and used.

The adolescent or immature person misunderstands this power to heal and to free energy as a magical or omnipotent state and tries to possess this level of being through fantasy or wishful thinking, confusing it with a manic "high." It is for this reason that the New Testament and much of the literature of Christian mysticism warns against the temptations of power; and it is for this reason that Buddhist literature is often of the puzzling negative mode, suggesting all the paths that are *not* the path of empathy and clarity. There is no self-inflation involved in the giving of the healer, no pride in giving, no division of awareness. Such signs are sure indications of anxiety in the giver, and of unsure vision.

The Buddhist formulation of the stages of purified vision is the formulation of a process of greater and greater security and concentration of vision, of converging modes of idea, sensation, feeling, and action—until the sensuous body, the crystal mind, and the golden smile express the imperturbable understanding and sympathetic serenity of empathic vision. At this level of concentration, powers of memory and illuminating intelligence make all situations the same, a field for the operation of compassionate giving. The fearless even-mindedness and freedom from the need enables the bodhisattva to descend into any situation with security. The healer can penetrate any level of development or mode of affliction without loss of self-shape, and this is the basis of unlimited empathy. The energy saved by the healer by his or her lack of involvement with the anxiety of survival becomes available for investment in the maturation process of others. Wherever such a healer finds himself or herself to be, there the spiral of growth, clarification, and maturation is energized.

The ideal of perfect empathic giving remains largely an ideal—in which form, on the highest level of integration—even dreams become a clear source of helping power, a resonator rather than a mere projection. But one can only give gifts commensurate with the state of internatl security achieved; and that is why anxiety reduction and the clarification of delusional forms of being is primary. The capacity to slay the dragons of fear reveals the world as it is—full of suffering people. Our struggle is to develop this point of view in ourselves, our families, our groups, and, finally, in the state.

SOCIAL SPACE: OUR CRITICAL TASKS

One of the critical tasks of our era is to socialize the gains of empathic development, to amplify them, and to multiply them. This can only be done through pairs and small groups supported by social networks, all dedicated to the reduction of the domain of fantasy in their areas, and to the expansion of safe space for everyone at every stage in the life cycle. Many groups are already doing this work, but they do not recognize each other or use a common language. As in individual therapy, and in marriage, the fear of integration is confused with the loss of identity, and it is a strong barrier to connection and a higher power of identity. Splitting interferes with integration at every level. Splitting begins as the taboo on seeing where and how the good object goes, as the repression of jealousy. Jealousy interferes with mutual recognition and cooperation—even among empathic groups.

The social parallel to the primal scene might be described as Father's Ownership of the Means of Production, or by Darwin as possession of the mating space—with the exclusion and inhibition of competitive onlookers. In the days of Zeus and Odin, the perception of the primal scene was blinding. Our relation to the primal scene governs our developmental position—from flight in nightmare terror, to self-blindness, to frozen inhibition, to the challenging voice, and the penetration of the forbidden zone of goods reserved for the gods. As in the Grail myth, however, only the eye of compassion can see how *all* suffer from divided goods, child, king, and God.

The reduction of idealization is the reduction of envy; and it opens our capacity to have sexual and social goods by being strong enough to work for them, penetrating resistances outside and inside the self, outside and inside the group. Like Odysseus, we must return home and repossess our goods, after a long exile and the winnowing of our hearts and minds.

But social space must now not be reserved only for the royal few. Once secure in our share of sexual and social good, we can share with others, outside life-and-death competition, guided by enlightened guilt and by sober understanding. The evolutionary drama in this theater of social ecology is the extension of sexual development to all, and its use as a base for psychosocial development. Genital sexuality, unlike infantile and adolescent forms, expresses surplus and security, safe space, and generative capability.

The paradox is simple: Only the full person, connected to all centers—mind, heart, speech, act, sex—is able to be empty of egotistical cravings to retrieve lost parts of the self from others—and so is in a position to receive and to give *as a self,* empathically. In this process of self-realization, growth converts the unnecessary surplus of sexual reproductive power into the necessary currency of *human* exchange—without using brutal mechanisms of inhibition.

Sexual powers become the powers of socialized love in an integrated individual. Having the self means security against forms of omnipotent fantasy—limitless wealth, power, or control. Completeness, the realization of self-hood, is the basis of generosity. Centering makes giving possible.

The doctrines of reincarnation, of hell-purgatory-heaven, and of neurosis and integration are the same: expressions of a positional dialectic of the stages of incarnation. We are all products of our path-following and our identifications. We all turn our faces to someone. All religious traditions agree on this self-process as a series of mirrorings of our models and our desires. We can feel safe only when we do not dread our own projections or our falling backward or downward into bestial, sinning positions—and when we do not envy, idealize, and devaluate those whose natures we feel powerless to emulate. We feel safe when we know ourselves to be like others. We are all struggling through the same stages of being, from birth to death.

Carl Jung, Erik Erikson, Otto Rank, Norman O. Brown, and Ernest Becker have done profound work on the desire for immortality as a denial of living as well as of dying. Our social task, like the task of a psychotherapist, is to expose the costs of such denials. Our private and public myths are attempts to contain our anxiety and to bridge our gaps of ignorance. But our understanding is growing in such a way that we have reduced the need to transfer responsibility for our living and dying to gods, culture heroes, or ideologies that will protect us against images of death or contact with the negative aspects of our selves. The more we can live in *this* life, the less we need to seek another.

History, as Ernest Becker has written, is a succession of immortality ideologies which guarantee the eternity and the goodness of a group, at the cost of projecting the bad onto another group. Such denial and omnipotence produces the paradox that evil is generated by the will to overcome death and evil. Failure to tolerate death and bad in the self and in the social body means that others must be eliminated, violated, and manipulated in the service of our ideology, so that we can remain ideal in our own eyes. Such betrayals of others and of our own selves emerge from the unconscious and pass into political forms. History becomes a corporate form of acting out on other groups. Only the acceptance of death and evil, in the self and in our own groups, can promise the end of history as a nightmare.

We are the same as others; others are like ourselves. All we can truly own is the even-mindedness of this compassionate understanding. Then we begin to understand the meaning of the simple message of Buddha, or Jesus, or Rumi, or Baal Shem—that we learn in order to give and receive, not to exploit or hoard. All guilt proceeds from the inability to give love, which alone is stronger than death or fear. Our loving and our knowing create safe space for the self—for all of the self. What we are struggling for is the creation of social forms that would clear safe space for all members of the human family.

Readings

BECKER, ERNEST, *Escape from Evil,* Free Press, New York.

BION, W. R., *Attention and Interpretation,* London, 1970.

BION, W. R., *Experiences in Groups,* New York, 1961.

BROWN, NORMAN O., *Life Against Death,* Vantage Books: New York, 1959.

DEMAUSE, LLOYD, *The History of Childhood,* New York, 1974.

DUBOS, RENE, *Man Adapting,* Yale, 1965.

EINSTEIN, ALBERT, *The Meaning of Relativity,* Princeton University Press, 1970 ed.

ERIKSON, ERIK, *Gandhi's Truth,* Hogarth Press, New York, 1969.

FREIBERG, SELMATT, *The Magic Years,* Scribner's, New York, 1959.

FREUD, SIGMUND, *Civilization and Its Discontents,* Vol. XXI, *Standard Edition of the Works of Sigmund Freud,* London, 1961.

FORNARI, FRANCO, *The Psychoanalysis of War,* New York, 1974.

FULLER, BUCKMINSTER, *Synergetics,* New York, 1975.

GOLDSTEIN, J., FREUD, A., SOLNIT, A. J., *Beyond the Best Interests of the Child,* New York, 1973.

GORINDA, LAMA ANAGARIKA, *Foundations of Tibetan Mysticism,* New York, 1969.

HALLE, LOUIS, J., *men and Nations,* Princeton, 1962.

HUIZINGA, J., *Homo Ludens,* Boston, 1955.

JAQUES, ELIOT, WORK, *Creativity and Social Justice,* New York, 1970.

JONES, RICHARD M., *The New Psychology of Dreams,* New York, 1970.

JUNG, C. G., *Symbols of Transformation,* Vol. V, *The Collected Works* of C. G. Jung, pantheon Books, 1956.

KELEMAN, STANLEY, *Living Your Dying,* New York, 1974.

KLEIN, MELANIE, *The Writings of Melanie Klein,* Vols. I-IV, London, 1975.

LAING, R. D., *The Divided Self,* Baltimore, 1969.

LING, KARL, *The Grundrisse,* ed. & trans. David McLellan, Harper & Row, 1971.

MAY, ROLLO, *Love and Will,* W. W. Norton, New York, 1969.

MELTZER, DONALD, *The Psycho-Analytical Process,* London, 1967.

NEUMANN, ERICH, *The Origins and History of Consciousness,* New York, 1954.

NISBET, ROBERT A., *Community and Power,* Oxford, 1962.

OLLMAN, BERTELL, *Alienation,* Cambridge, 1971.

PIAGET, JEAN, *The Child and Reality,* New York, 1973.

RANK, OTTO, *The Myth of the Birth of the Hero,* Vintage Books, New York, 1959.

REICH, WILHELM, *The Mass Psychology of Fascism,* trans. J. R. Cartagno, New York, 1959.

SHAPIRO, S. AND TYRKA, H., *Trusting Yourself: Psychotherapy as a Beginning,* Prentice-Hall, Spectrum Books, New York, 1975.

SZASZ, THOMAS S., *The Manufacture of Madness,* New York, 1970.

WHITEHEAD, ALFRED NORTH, *Process and Reality,* Humanities Press, New York, 1955.

WILLIAMS, WILLIAM A., *The Great Evasion,* Chicago, 1964.

WYNNE-EDWARDS, V. C., *Animal Dispersion in Relation to Social Behavior,* New York, 1972.